"Dr Calhoun, a pioneer in the field, has produced a clear and concise primer for the threat assessment and management community. This work will serve the needs of those new to the field and as a ready reference for those familiar with his past work. This primer should be added to the tool kit of anyone who needs to deal with threatening or disturbing situations in any environment."

Stephen W. Weston,
Co-*Author of* Threat Assessment
and Management Strategies

"Including a discussion of the distinction between those threatening violence and those focused on committing violence (hunters v. howlers) is a useful and necessary feature for the text and will help readers in making important determinations in real world contexts. Introducing the path to intended violence is a critical addition to the proposed text and will help readers establish a solid understanding of this critical foundational element of broader threat assessment practices in an applied environment."

Jason R. Jolicoeur, Ph.D.,
Minnesota State University, Mankato

"The major issue in managing threats is the lack of early identification and reporting of concerns. This book addresses this issue and seeks to introduce a new process that encourages increased reporting. A major strength is the author, whose reputation and credibility stands out."

Philip Grindell, *Defuse Global*

I0130323

Effective Threat Management

Effective Threat Management: A Primer presents the ABCs for identifying, assessing, and managing potentially violent individuals. By offering practical advice and tactics for dealing with problem individuals, the *Primer* serves as an ideal reference source for threat management professionals and as a practical introduction to threat management best practices for those new to the field. The question-and-answer format makes finding information easy. The book offers tips and cautions on practical ways to implement an effective threat management program in various situations, such as interpersonal relationships, schools, workplaces, public gathering places, or religious establishments. The *Primer* emphasizes practical, field-tested approaches to the challenges of identifying, assessing, and managing problem individuals.

In the *Primer*, author Frederick S. Calhoun, a respected expert in threat assessment and management, shows how to set up a threat management process free of elaborate procedures or significant commitments of resources. The *Primer* offers a practical, step-by-step process for identifying, assessing, and managing problem individuals. Each section answers specific questions. A quick reference guide allows users to quickly locate specific issues or topics. Text boxes throughout the *Primer* offer practical support, helpful cautions, and real case-study illustrations.

This user-friendly book will help threat management professionals in law enforcement and security positions as well as other professionals potentially facing threats, such as mental health practitioners, teachers, HR professionals, small business owners, and anyone else confronted with the need for threat management.

Frederick S. Calhoun created and managed the national workplace violence prevention program for the US Transportation Security Administration (TSA), an agency with a workforce of over 50,000 employees. He implemented the workplace violence prevention policy, created the training program for all employees, and managed specific incidents involving potential workplace violence. Calhoun earned a Ph.D. from the University of Chicago. During the 1990s, he was the lead researcher and principal architect in developing the threat assessment process used by the US Marshals Service for analyzing risks to federal judicial officials. Calhoun has conducted hundreds of training seminars on threat management. With co-author Stephen W. Weston, Calhoun wrote five books on threat management. Calhoun continues to teach a periodic two-day seminar, "Managing Threats: Reducing the Risk of Violence," designed to train law enforcement officers, mental health professionals, and private security officials in identifying, assessing, and managing individuals of violent intent.

Effective Threat Management

A Primer

Frederick S. Calhoun

R Routledge
Taylor & Francis Group

NEW YORK AND LONDON

Designed cover image: © Getty Images

First published 2025
by Routledge
605 Third Avenue, New York, NY 10158

and by Routledge
4 Park Square, Milton Park, Abingdon, Oxon, OX14 4RN

Routledge is an imprint of the Taylor & Francis Group, an informa business

© 2025 Frederick S. Calhoun

ISBN: 978-1-032-89528-4 (hbk)
ISBN: 978-1-032-89526-0 (pbk)
ISBN: 978-1-003-54328-2 (ebk)

DOI: 10.4324/9781003543282

Typeset in Sabon
by KnowledgeWorks Global Ltd.

To Debra, again – and always.

Contents

10 Managing   67

Acknowledgements

I thank Tyson Bailey, Philip Grindell, Jason Jolicouer, Vicki King, Amy McCorkill, Kris Mohandie, and David Upchurch for their perceptive comments and suggestions as I drafted this book. Their recommendations greatly improved it. Any errors remain entirely my own.

Steve Weston, my long-time collaborator, offered useful suggestions and edits to early drafts of the book. As always, I am grateful for his insights. The ideas, approaches, and concepts distilled in the *Primer* come directly from our work together. More than that, though, I greatly appreciate all the fun we've had over the years. So far, we've laughed our way through five books and numerous articles, as well as scores of training seminars. Our partnership has been a highlight of my career. I look forward to future collaborations.

Thanks, too, to Naima Brown, vice president for Student Affairs, and her colleagues at Sante Fe College in Gainesville, Florida. They invited me to teach a six-hour seminar on threat management to nearly 50 threat management practitioners from Sante Fe College and nine neighboring organizations. Doing so allowed me to try out the question-and-answer format used in the *Primer* as well as to gauge how practicing threat assessment professionals responded to the ideas and approaches outlined here. It proved to be a most rewarding experience from which I learned a lot.

My children, Austin, Emily, Amy, and their families are living proof that happy, well-adjusted individuals continue to roam the earth. They all serve me well as living reminders of that fact.

For many reasons, I owe my deepest thanks to my wife, Debra. During all we went through while I worked on this book, Debra's practical wisdom, patient support, and great good humor got us to the other side. Her comments, suggestions, questions, and critiques forced me to clarify my ideas and their expression. Debra made the book possible, but even more, she makes life worthwhile.

Chapter 1

Overview

What is Effective Threat Management?
What is an effective threat management process?
How will the Primer *help?*

What Is *Effective Threat Management?*

Effective Threat Management: A Primer presents the *ABC*s of identifying, assessing, and managing potentially violent individuals. Those three steps – identify, assess, and manage – define the threat management process. The goal of that process centers on managing a problem individual – the Subject – away from acts of violence or disruption. The *Primer* serves as both a ready reference for professionals and a "how-to" guide for those new to the field. It introduces basic concepts and approaches for effectively implementing a threat management process. The *Primer* essentially distills the ideas and approaches Stephen W. Weston and I described in *Concepts and Case Studies in Threat Management*[1] and *Threat Assessment and Management Strategies*, 1st.[2] and 2nd eds.[3] In doing so, it presents the material in an easily accessible format designed for practical use by anyone confronted with the challenge of managing problem individuals.

Scope of the Primer

This *Primer* caters to those with some threat management training as well as to newcomers to the field. It emphasizes practical strategies for preventing violence. The *Primer*:

- Reviews the threat management fundamentals;
- Describes in detail the processes for identifying, assessing, and managing potential violence; and
- Concludes with a brief review of the pitfalls threat managers face.

DOI: 10.4324/9781003543282-1

Practical Focus

The *Primer* focuses on practical ideas and approaches for dealing with problem individuals who may pose a threat to other individuals, groups, or locations. It offers useful, field-tested strategies and tactics. The *Primer* eschews jargon, useless theories, impractical approaches, and incomprehensible statistical analyses. Instead, it helps readers roll up their sleeves and get to work thwarting those individuals intent on violence as well as those individuals seeking to inspire fear or chaos. Threat managers must manage both types of problem individuals.

What Is an Effective Threat Management Process?

An effective threat management process readily identifies, assesses, and manages problem individuals coming to the threat manager's attention. It does not require elaborate procedures or significant commitments of resources. While teams of subject-matter experts remain the ideal, smaller organizations can still benefit from acknowledging the need for a threat management process and implementing its fundamentals. The process begins with identifying a "designated threat receiver" who takes the responsibility for overseeing the threat management process. Using this *Primer* can help that receiver set up the appropriate means for responding to problem situations as they arise.

How Will the *Primer* Help?

Using the *Primer* will help establish a practical threat management program tailored to the reader's particular environment and needs as well as answer specific questions threat managers may have when dealing with situations. The complexity of the program depends on the scope of the problem and the risk level of the environment. Controversial or highly public organizations such as Microsoft or Planned Parenthood need dedicated threat managers and sophisticated threat management programs. Smaller institutions and local businesses probably do not. All of them, however, face the risk of angry customers or patrons, disgruntled current or former employees, or violent domestic partners targeting someone in the organization. That common risk requires some level of threat management, however simple. This *Primer* can help set up a straightforward, yet effective threat management process.

Using the Primer

Each section of the *Primer* opens with specific questions which that section addresses. A quick reference guide at the front gives users a way to quickly find specific issues or topics. Text boxes throughout the *Primer* provide case studies, more detailed explanations of key concepts, or various cautions. Readers may use the *Primer* as a step-by-step guide for setting up a threat management program or they may simply refer to it for answers to specific issues or concerns.

Why Threat Management?

According to *Washington Post* reporter Justine McDaniel, at least 70% of the shooters in the deadliest mass killings in 2023 engaged in behaviors that caused concern among their families, friends, or law enforcement *before* they launched their attacks. The Subjects "had made previous threats, been violent, alarmed family members or signaled their intentions online." According to one expert in gun violence quoted in the article, "Very rarely do we see someone commit a mass shooting where there were no warning signs." Another violence expert told McDaniel that "a very high proportion of mass shooters leak their intentions in advance. What that does is it creates opportunities … for intervention and de-escalation." As with mass shooters, so, too, most other attackers. Individuals who intend to commit a violent act behave in ways that can be detected. Threat management uses that detection to disrupt their plans.[1]

A 2015 FBI report noted that "lack of knowledge – knowledge about threat assessment and management itself, about risk factors and warning signs, about what goes into managing potential targets" is the "first and foremost fundamental potential barrier" to identifying, assessing, and managing individuals posing a risk of violence.[2]

Because individuals intending violence engage in noticeable behaviors, their intentions can be disrupted and they can be diverted from acts of violence *if those who notice the behaviors know what they mean and where to report their concerns so that the Subject can be stopped.* Why threat management? Because an effective threat management process offers the best way to prevent Subjects intending violence from carrying out their violent act.

Notes:

1 Justine McDaniel, "Gunmen in 7 of 2023's Deadliest Mass Killing Showed Warning Signs," *Washington Post*, November 4, 2023, retrieved at https://www.washingtonpost.com/nation/2023/11/04/mass-shootings-warnings-maine-red-flag/.

2 Molly Ammon, *et al.*, *Making Prevention a Reality: Identifying, Assessing, and Managing the Threat of Targeted Attacks*, Federal Bureau of Investigation, Behavioral Threat Assessment Center, Quantico, VA, 2015.

Notes

1 Frederick S. Calhoun and Stephen W. Weston, *Concepts and Case Studies in Threat Management* (Boca Raton, FL: CRC Press, 2013).
2 Frederick S. Calhoun and Stephen W. Weston, *Threat Assessment and Management Strategies: Identifying the Howlers and Hunters* (Boca Raton, FL: CRC Press, 2009).
3 Frederick S. Calhoun and Stephen W. Weston, *Threat Assessment and Management Strategies: Identifying the Howlers and Hunters*, 2nd ed. (Boca Raton, FL: CRC Press, 2016).

Part I

Threat Management Fundamentals

Chapter 2

Subjects of Concern

Who needs managing?
What is involved in effectively managing Subjects of Concern?
Who are Hunters and Howlers?

Who Needs Managing?

Threat management deals with problem individuals who may pose a risk, especially in terms of:

- Violence
- Disruption

Threat managers refer to these individuals as *Subjects of Concern.*

What Is Involved in Effectively Managing Subjects of Concern?

Effectively managing Subjects of Concern requires addressing several key questions:

- Definition: What criteria define threats and inappropriate communications?
- Identification: Who is the Subject of Concern?
- Assessment: Is the Subject of Concern on the Path to Intended Violence?
- Environment: In which venue does the Subject of Concern perceive themselves?
- Inhibitors: What inhibitors are in play?

DOI: 10.4324/9781003543282-3

Who Are Hunters and Howlers?

Subjects of Concern generally fall into one of two types:

1 *Hunters:* Individuals who actively intend violence and who take concrete steps toward that goal.
2 *Howlers:* Individuals who want to frighten or emotionally connect with their target, but who take no steps toward a violent act.

Table 2.1 compares hunters to howlers.

Table 2.1 Hunters Versus Howlers

Hunters	Howlers
Engage in attack-related behaviors.	Engage in attention-seeking behaviors.
Pose physical risk of violence.	Pose risk of emotional distress.

The Cases of the Original Hunter and the Original Howler

A dedicated amateur hunter, Jack McKnight, believed the federal government had declared war on him. Arrested for growing marijuana on his Kansas farm and charged with owning firearms while intending to sell the illegal weed, McKnight faced a ten-year prison sentence without the possibility of probation or parole. On the day scheduled for sentencing, McKnight armed himself with three pistols and a couple dozen pipe bombs. He towed his pickup truck to the county sheriff's office where he used pipe bombs to blow the truck up. He then drove to the Topeka federal courthouse, blew up the car, then shot and killed the Court Security Officer staffing the magnetometer at the entrance to the federal court. He exploded several more pipe bombs as he walked to the clerk's office where he barricaded himself. When police failed to respond quickly enough, McKnight shot himself in the head.

McKnight became the prototype for hunters. He stood for all those individuals who intended to commit a violent act.

Ray F. wrote letters to federal judges across the United States. The letters described in intimate detail Ray's intention to kill the judge, slaughter the judge's family, and otherwise terrorize the judicial official. Ray did not know the judges to whom he wrote, they did not preside over his trial nor have anything to do with his incarceration in the Bureau of Prisons' mental hospital. As Ray once explained to his doctors, he would not know what to do with himself all day if he did not have his letters to write. For Ray, writing letters threatening judges was a hobby, a way to pass the time while serving a dreary prison sentence.

Ray F. became the prototype for howlers. He stood for all those individuals who intended to disturb or frighten their victims, but who lacked the wherewithal – or the nerve – to carry out their threats.

Source: Frederick S. Calhoun, *Hunters and Howlers: Threats and Violence Against Federal Judicial Officials, 1789–1993*, United States Marshals Service, Arlington, VA, 1998, pp. xvii–xix.

Manage Both Hunters and Howlers

Both hunters and howlers require managing. Since hunters intend violence, they usually demand the threat manager's immediate attention, but howlers should never be ignored or set aside. They cause serious emotional stress on their targets. They also pose the risk of becoming hunters. Threat managers need to manage both types of Subjects proactively.

Caution

Managing howlers requires vigilance against taking

any *action* or *inaction*

that might result in transforming a howler into a hunter.

Figure 2.1 provides a typology for howlers, dividing them between Personal Howlers, who personally know their targets, and Impersonal Howlers, who have never met their targets. Both types are further divided between those who threaten harm to their targets and those who merely seek a relationship. As the figure shows, within those broad divisions lie a host of different motivations. The figure also lists each howler's distinguishing characteristics.

Types of Howlers

Personal
Knows Target

Impersonal
Does Not Know Target

Personal — Knows Target

Sinister — *Threatens Harm*

Controller
Seeks Control Over Target
Recognizable by their:
- Focus on Intimate Partner
- Target Readily Available
- Use Intimate Knowledge About Target
- Insistence on Controlling Target

Intimidator
Seeks to Intimidate
Recognizable by their:
- Focus on Coworkers, Classmates, or Similar Personal Relationships.
- Purpose to frighten or Discomfit Target
- Use of Personal Knowledge About Target
- Target Accessible
- Use Intimidation to Affect Target Behavior

Dirty Trickster
Shifts Blame to Third Party
Recognizable by their:
- Use of Specific Information on Who Threatened
- Lack of Issue Between Target and Subject

Binder — *Seeks Relationship*

Seeker
Seeks Intimate Relationship
Recognizable by their:
- Focus on Specific Individual Who Rejected Subject's Advances
- Expressed Desire for Closer Relationship Over Target's Objections
- Persistent Attempts to Contact Target

Maintainer
Seeks to Reestablish Intimate Relationship
Recognizable by their:
- Focus on Target Who Ended Their Relationship
- Detailed Familiarity with Target
- References to Past Times Together
- Use of Multiple Methods of Communication

Deluder
Suffers Deluded Belief They Have or Had Intimate Relationship
Recognizable by their:
- Focus on Nonexistent Relationship.
- References to Nonexistent Relationship
- Delusions or Out of Touch with Reality.
- Persistent Pursuit of Target.

Impersonal — Does Not Know Target

Sinister — *Threatens Harm*

Self-Defender
Feels Under Attack
Recognizable by their:
- Focus on Specific Issue
- Desire for Target to Fix Issue
- Use of Threats
- Refusal to Take Responsibility
- Insistence on Resolution on Subject's Terms

Celebrity Seeker
Attracted by Target's Public Figure Status
Recognizable by their:
- Focus on Celebrity as Celebrity
- Lack of Personal Knowledge About Target
- Animosity Over Target's Fame
- Image of Subject Better Than Target

Habitual
Making Threats Is a Hobby
Recognizable by their:
- Voluminous Communications
- No Personal Motive
- Emphasis on Threats and Violence
- Evidence of Mental Illness
- Makes Multiple Threats

Crusader
Threatens for Some Personal Cause
Recognizable by their:
- Focus on Issues
- Making Issue Larger Than Themselves
- Portraying Themselves as Part of Group
- Justify Their Behavior By Importance of Their Cause

Copycat
Inspired by Acts of Violence
Recognizable by their:
- Focus on Recent Violence
- Claims of Violent Tactics
- Harmless Copying of Well-Known Violent Act

Delusional
Mental Delusion Compelling Threats
Recognizable by Their:
- Focus on Imaginary Perception of Target
- Belief Target a Threat to Subject or Others
- Insists Target Is Someone Else

Binder — *Seeks Relationship*

Relationship
Seeks Bond with Celebrity
Recognizable by their:
- Focus on Public Figure
- Belief Communications Bonded Subject and Target.
- Claims Being Best or Closest Defender of Target.
- Believes Subject and Target Have True Connection.

Delusory
Believes in Relationship with Target
Recognizable by their:
- Focus on Nonexistent Relationship with Target.
- Claims Receiving Messages from Target.
- Insistence Target Reciprocates.
- Evidence of Mental Illness.

Callow
Don't Get How Inappropriate They Are
Recognizable by their:
- Expectation Target Will Reply
- Nonviolent Motive and Intentions.
- Insists on Acting on Expectation

Figure 2.1 Types of Howlers by Perceived Relationship and Intent

Chapter 3

The Two Paths to Violence

What are the two paths to violence?
What behaviors are associated with the path to intended violence?

What Are the Two Paths to Violence?

Violent interactions follow two distinct, though similar, paths. One route involves impulsive behavior, the other entails deliberate acts. On the one hand, *impromptu violence* occurs impulsively, usually prompted by an unanticipated interaction between the Subject and the target. *Intended violence*, on the other hand, results from a premeditated, purposeful decision by the Subject to act violently. Both paths have identifiable milestones associated with particular behaviors. The paths to violence help threat managers locate where a Subject may be in terms of moving toward a violent act.

Impromptu Violence

Impromptu violence occurs when the Subject reacts emotionally to some perceived insult, injury, or threat. It takes place in that moment, without much thought or hesitation. It is a violent eruption driven by the emotions spawned by the perceived slight. The Subject feels some insult or injustice and reacts immediately. The Subject gets cut off in traffic or loses patience with the loudmouth at the bar or takes offense at his team's sudden loss. They lose their temper or act impulsively. Without taking the time to think through their actions, the Subject retaliates with whatever weapon lies close to hand, such as their car, beer bottle, or fists. Most importantly, the Subject did not plan or premeditate the violence. It arose out of the heat of the moment.

Intended Violence

Intended violence proceeds methodically, without the sense of immediacy that accompanies impromptu violence. Like impromptu violence, the Subject feels some grievance, a real or imagined sense of injury or insult. They

DOI: 10.4324/9781003543282-4

Path to Impromptu Violence

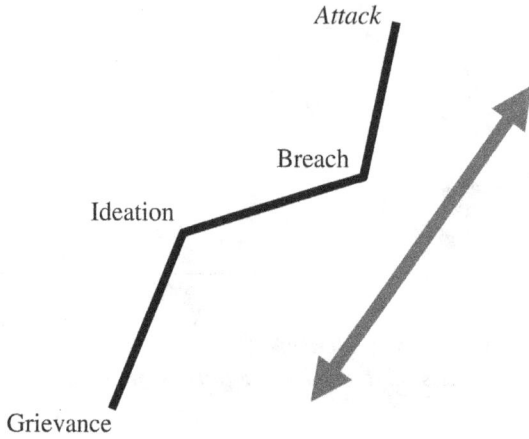

Figure 3.1 Path to Impromptu Violence

then decide that violence is the only way to relieve the wrong done to them. From that idea, the Subject takes the time to figure out how to carry out the attack. This often involves researching the target, developing a plan, and then preparing for the attack according to the dictates of the plan. As in impromptu violence, the last two steps in the process of intended violence consist of breaching the target's security and attacking.

Path to Intended Violence

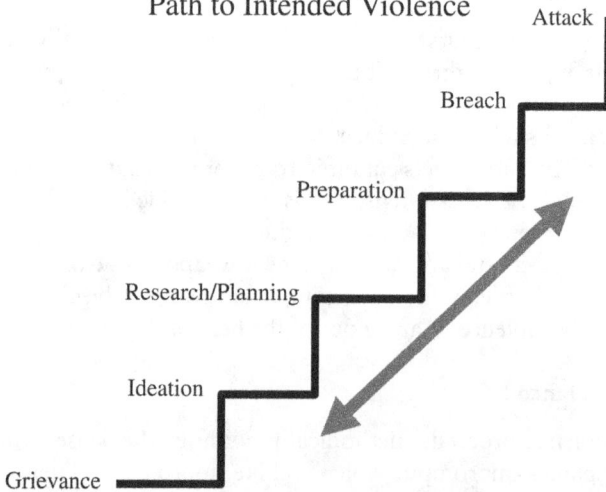

Figure 3.2 Path to Intended Violence

Moving Along the Path to Intended Violence

The Subject may move back and forth along the path, changing their mind or adapting their plans to fit changing circumstances. The amount of research, planning, and preparation depends on how much the Subject already knows about their potential target. Domestic partners, for example, need little research because they already know their partners' habits, routines, places of work, home address, and other information conducive to planning an assault. Conversely, Subjects focused on public figures may know little about the target's accessibility. The Subject may already own a weapon or other equipment called for in the plan, thus simplifying their preparations. The level of security around the target also affects how much research the Subject needs to conduct. In sum, the Subject's movements along the path to intended violence depend entirely on the situation at hand. Using the concept of the path requires the threat manager to account for the context and circumstances of the situation.

More About
How Subjects Move Along the Path to Intended Violence

A Subject's movements along the path to intended violence depend entirely on the situation at hand. Subjects may move fast or slow, use prior target knowledge as their research and planning, or rely on current weapons possession for preparation. They may turn around, hesitate, return years later, or otherwise customize the process to suit their needs. Although they go through all the motions, they do so at their own pace and in their own way.

Search for Justice

As with impromptu violence, intended violence may stem from a perceived injustice or offense, but the aggrieved party takes the time and effort to plan and prepare for the culminating violent act. Time means little on the path to intended violence. Indeed, time's role may only appear if the Subject settles on some particular calendar date for its symbolic or practical importance.

What Behaviors Are Associated With the Path to Intended Violence?

Specific behaviors define each step along the path, thus making them noticeable and thereby manageable. Table 3.1 lists some of the types of behaviors associated with each milestone along the path to intended violence.

Table 3.1 Types of Behaviors Along the Path to Intended Violence

Grievance	Sense of injustice: • Mission • Loss • Destiny • Revenge • Infamy
Ideation	References to: • Violence • Other attacks or attackers • Weapons • Important date
Research/planning	Behaviors such as: • Stalking • Suspicious inquiries • Information gathering • Surveillance • Exploring security
Preparation	Actions such as: • Acquiring or attempting to acquire weapon • Assembling equipment • Final acts • Wearing specific clothing • Observing significant date
Breach	Movements such as: • Getting around security • Lethal approach • Stealthy approach
Attack	Moment when: • Assault launched

Grievance

Understanding a Subject's grievance often proves difficult or impossible. They remain uniquely personal to the individual and may make little or no sense to anyone else. A "reasonable person" standard does not apply. The sense of outrage usually entails a strong emotional investment by the Subject, which means the complaint has no time limit or expiration date. The Subject, too, may hide or obscure their motivation. Since everyone, at one time or another, develops a grievance over something, having a grievance does not prove the Subject has launched themselves on the path to intended violence. That momentous step comes with Ideation.

The Case of the Inner Voices
Grievance

Sometime around February 2023, Robert Card went through a "bad breakup" with the woman he met playing cornhole at Schemengees Bar & Grille in Lewiston, Maine. At the same time, Card began wearing hearing aids for the first time. He told family members that unknown voices in his head warned him that someone from Schemengees and the Just-In-Time bowling alley broadcast messages on the internet labeling Card a pedophile. In July, while on a training exercise with his Army Reserve unit at West Point, New York, Card suddenly accused several of his fellow soldiers of also calling him a pedophile. His commanding officer ordered him to a local mental institution where he stayed for two weeks. Card remained outraged at the false accusations. The injustice continued to grate on him.

Ideation

Arriving at the conclusion that only violence can resolve the Subject's grievance is a watershed, the point at which the Subject determines to resolve their grievance through violent action. The decision prompts changes in their behavior and demeanor. They may become more focused, intense, and specific. The Subject may wrap themselves in a feeling of grandiosity, transforming their simple grievance into a larger issue or cause. This might show in more violent language or actions, or they might keep their plans hidden to avoid being stopped.

The Case of the Inner Voices Continued
Ideation

After internal voices began warning Card that others had published messages on the internet accusing him of pedophilia, Card told his brother he thought of carrying out a mass shooting. In September 2023, seven or eight months later, Card told a fellow soldier he intended "to shoot up the drill center at Saco" where his company was based, and he would "get" the officers who ordered him to the mental hospital in New York.

Research and Planning

How much research the Subject needs to conduct depends entirely on the situation. The more intimate the relationship between the Subject and the target, the less the Subject needs to delve into the target's habits, routines, and personal life. They know them already. Conversely, the less interpersonal the relationship, the more information the Subject needs to dig up. Intimate relationships and workplace and school settings need less research since the Subject knows the target, works at the site, or attends the school. Other targets, such as public figures, gathering places, or representative targets may require the Subject to make suspicious inquiries, conduct surveillance, engage in stalking, or otherwise take observable steps to gather information. The threat manager may confidently deduce the Subject's prior knowledge about the target by knowing the Subject's relationship to the target.

Information readily available on the internet allows Subjects to conduct their research in private, thus making the threat manager's ability to find evidence of that research infinitely more complicated. One way to counteract that challenge is for the threat manager to routinely do their own internet searches to determine what is available about the potential target. Although that will not prove what the Subject may know, it will at least inform the threat manager about potential weaknesses or exposure in the target's security.

The Case of the Inner Voices Continued
Research and Planning

Card liked to hang out at the Just-In-Time bowling alley and Schemengees Bar & Grille, which were 4 miles away from each other. His familiarity with both allowed him to make plans for his attack without the need for conducting overt surveillance or scouting missions. His September threat to "shoot up" the drill center at Saco, another site he frequently went to, may indicate he had not settled on a final target as late as a month before when he launched his attack on the bowling alley and bar. Whatever his final target, his knowledge of those three locations gave him plenty of information to draw on in making his plans.

Preparation

Based on the Subject's plan of attack, the Subject needs to prepare for the actual assault. Like the plan itself, preparations may be simple or elaborate. They involve such behaviors as acquiring a weapon, assembling equipment, arranging transportation, observing significant or symbolic dates, costuming, or – if the Subject does not expect to survive the assault – conducting final-act behaviors (giving away possessions, compiling a last will, making final arrangements). Preparing themselves marks the transition from planning to implementing. Increases in intensity and momentum usually accompany that shift. And perhaps for the first time, preparations may require observable attack-related behaviors.

As with research and planning, information available on the internet makes the Subject's preparations easier. The threat manager should therefore conduct their own internet searches to identify vulnerabilities and potential weaknesses involving the target. Also, always check the Subject's background, weapons ownership, and familiarity with weapons. These provide valuable information about the Subject's access and abilities.

The Case of the Inner Voices Continued
Preparation

Although Robert Card already owned 10–15 firearms, in early July he purchased a Small-Frame Autoloading Rifle, or SFAR for short. The rifle is like the better-known AR-15, except it fires a more powerful .308 caliber round compared to the standard 5.56 mm round for the AR-15. Because of the more powerful ammunition, SFARs can be used for big game hunting. The rifle comes with a 20-round magazine.

Breach

Breach entails the Subject getting past the target's security – however elaborate or primitive that may be – and making the lethal approach. Waylaying the target may occur openly or in secret. Whether a letter bomb or a simple physical assault, ambush, or frontal attack, the Subject needs to get close enough to the target to inflict the damage. Breach may rely on a specific window of opportunity based on the target's availability or the Subject's personal calendar. It may also depend on whether the Subject plans to escape after the attack or simply die trying. Isolating breach as a separate step recognizes that the Subject has a few final seconds to change their mind about carrying out the assault. Those few seconds also allow the target or the target's security time to thwart the attack.

The Case of the Inner Voices Continued
Breach

Just before 7:00 p.m. on October 25, Card drove to the Just-In-Time bowling alley, parked his car, and, with SFAR in hand, he opened the door and entered the building. As a public place, the bowling alley had no security perimeter. Minutes later, his business there done, Card returned to his car, drove around 4 miles to the south and west where he again parked his car in the parking lot and, SFAR in hand, let himself into Schemengees Bar & Grille, another public place with no security perimeter.

Attack

Attack is the last step along the path, the point when the Subject commits the violence. It also represents the failure of the threat management process.

The Case of the Inner Voices
Attack

Upon entering both Just-In-Time and Schemengees, Card began randomly shooting anyone who caught his attention. He killed seven people at the bowling alley, eight individuals at the bar. He then drove away. After a two-day search involving scores of law enforcement and Army personnel, they found Card's body in a trailer next to a recycling center in nearby Lisbon, Maine. Card had shot himself.

Sources: Jimmy Vielkind, "Dire Warning Signs About Maine Gunman Didn't Stop His Rampage," *Wall Street Journal,* October 31, 2023, retrieved at https://www.wsj.com/us-news/maine-shooting-robert-card-warnings-3673548e?reflink=integratedwebview_share; Shaila Dewan, Nicholas Bogel-Burroughs, and Chelsia Rose Marcius, "The Signs Were All There. Why Did No One Stop the Maine Shooter?" *New York Times,* November 2, 2023, retrieved at https://www.nytimes.com/2023/11/02/us/maine-shooting-mental-health-laws.html.

More About
Moving Along the Path to Intended Violence

- Time is not a factor along the path.
- Subject may move up or down the path.
- More intimate the relationship between Subject and target, less research and planning.
- Internet tools for research and planning complicate detection.
- Subject may already have all or some of the materials called for in their plan, thus simplifying their preparations.
- The split seconds between breach and attack give time for the Subject to change their mind or for the target or the target's security to disrupt the attack.

The threat manager should keep all these factors in mind when assessing whether or not the Subject has embarked on the path to intended violence.

Chapter 4

Threats and Inappropriate Communications

What are inappropriate communications or contacts?
What are the different types of threats?
What is the Intimacy Effect?
How do I determine a threat's credibility?

What Are Inappropriate Communications or Contacts?

Inappropriate communications or contacts involve unwanted interactions between the Subject and their target. They involve actions that convey disturbing, unsettling, or unpleasant messages. Inappropriate communications may not be threatening. They can be questionable, sinister, or otherwise suspicious. They may express infatuation, sexual interest, past relationships (real or imaginary), or a desire for a future relationship. They usually make the target feel uncomfortable or uneasy.

What Are the Different Types of Threats?

Threats fall within the broader category of inappropriate communications. They consist of any communication or contact that, directly or indirectly, warns of future physical harm. In effect, they promise some upcoming violent event. Subjects use threats to influence or control their target's behavior or to express anger or hostility. Generally, howlers make threats because they cause emotional disturbance or disruption. Hunters who focus on public figures tend to avoid using them since making a threat essentially reveals their plans. Subjects in closer interpersonal relationships may use threats to control their partner's behavior. As long as the threats work, the Subject has no reason to carry them out. Violence may follow when the target no longer obeys the conditions of the threat.

DOI: 10.4324/9781003543282-5

Caution

All threats are inappropriate

But

Not all inappropriate communications are threats.

Table 4.1 Types of Threats

Type of threat	Definition	Example
Direct	Clearly stated intention by Subject to harm target.	"I'm going to kill you."
Conditional	Risk of harm dependent on some action or inaction by the target.	"If you don't meet my demands, I'll hurt you."
Veiled	Communication unclear as to either Subject or harm.	"Someone someday is really going to make you pay for what you did."
Third party	Subject suggests another individual will carry out the actual harm.	"You know, one of these days somebody's really going to take this place out."
Disavowed or denied threat	Statements referencing harm while disclaiming intention to carry it out.	"I am not a violent person, but if I was, I would beat you within an inch of your life."
Threatening/ inappropriate contact	Physical gestures or behavior by Subject directed at target.	Information received that someone followed target home.

What Is the *Intimacy Effect?*

The *Intimacy Effect* suggests that the seriousness of a threat as an indicator of future violence depends on the interpersonal relationship between the Subject and their target. The closer that relationship, the more credible the threat.

Figure 4.1 illustrates the *Intimacy Effect.*

INTIMACY EFFECT

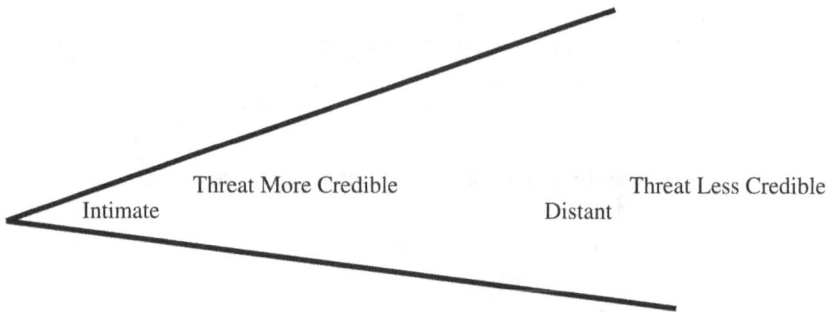

Threat More Credible   Threat Less Credible
    Intimate   Distant

Figure 4.1 The *Intimacy Effect*

The Case of the Disgruntled Grad Student

Murad Dervish never fit in with the faculty and fellow graduate students at the University of Arizona's Hydrology and Atmospheric Sciences Department. Faculty members complained that, from November 2021 until October 2022, Dervish harassed four professors, a female undergraduate, and the Dean of Students. He particularly singled out Professor Thomas Meixner for giving him a low grade on his Fall 2021 midterm. When the school denied giving Dervish information related to his upcoming expulsion hearing, the disgruntled grad student e-mailed the Dean of Students demanding the information. "If you don't I promise the consequences are going to be absolutely catastrophic," Dervish wrote, "I don't think you have any clue who you are dealing with but you are about to find out and I really don't think youre (sic) going to like it." On October 5, the expelled grad student returned to campus looking for Professor Meixner. "I knew you were going to do this," Meixner exclaimed after Dervish fatally shot him.

Sources: Ryan Quinn, "Faculty: Repeated Threats Unheeded, Professor Murdered," *Inside Higher Education*, February 1, 2023, retrieved at https://www.insidehighered.com/news/2023/02/02/report-warnings-ignored-u-ariz-professor-killed; Phil Andrew, "Review of the University of Arizona's Safety and Security Environment," March 24, 2023, retrieved at https://www.arizona.edu/sites/default/files/2023-03/PAX_Group_Report.pdf.

How Do I Determine a Threat's Credibility?

On the one hand, the *Intimacy Effect* means that threats become more believable (i.e., the Subject actually intends to take the promised action) when they happen between individuals who know each other (i.e., spouses, friends, or neighbors) or who happen to be in close physical proximity to each other, such as attending the same school or working at the same place. On the other hand, threats become less believable – or credible – when directed at public figures, such as the president, governor, or a celebrity. Regardless of the threat's credibility, threats should always be taken seriously and assessed in the context in which they occur. They should never be ignored if for no other reason than they may violate the law.

Threat managers should also recognize the difference between direct threats and "leakage," a term coined by FBI agent Mary O'Toole to describe the incidents in which the Subject discussed, referred to, or implied to others that they intended to commit violence against someone or something. Leakage frequently occurred prior to school and workplace incidents. It has also taken place before other acts of violence. Whereas direct threats are made by the Subject directly to the target, leakage involves a third party to whom the Subject confides or lets slip their plans. In "The Case of the Disgruntled Grad Student," Dervish threatened the Dean of Students; in "The Case of the Inner Voices," Card engaged in leakage when he told his brother he thought about carrying out a mass shooting and when he mentioned to a fellow soldier he intended "to shoot up the drill center at Saco."

The Case of the Seven Threatening Phone Calls

Joe Morelli lived alone with bipolar disorder in Endicott, NY, spending his days watching left-leaning television talk shows. On March 3, 2022, at 8:30 in the evening, Morelli saw a campaign ad featuring U.S. Congresswoman Marjorie Taylor Greene firing a .50 caliber sniper rifle at a Toyota Prius with the word "SOCIALISM" plastered in large type on the side. With Greene's second shot, the car exploded. "I'm going to blow away the Democrats' socialist agenda," Greene promised. Since the disability benefits Morelli depended on struck him as a form of socialism, Greene's ad made him feel ashamed. The ad prompted Morelli to Google the phone number of Greene's congressional office. Between 8:32 and 1:10 the next morning, Morelli left seven voice mails, spelling out his name and leaving his phone number – and threatening to physically harm the congresswoman.

On March 16, FBI agents arrested Morelli at his apartment. He admitted making the phone calls, which he only vaguely remembered making, but assured the agents that "I've never owned a weapon. I'm not going to freakin' D.C. and crap. I barely leave my house." The court sentenced Morelli to three months in prison. He served 81 days.

But that wasn't enough for the U.S. Attorney's office. The prosecutor requested restitution for Congresswoman Greene, claiming that in response to Morelli's threat, she spent $66,257.49 on security camera upgrades and a new fence. On the victim impact statement signed by Greene, she indicated that she felt unsafe, anxious, fearful, and angry in reaction to the threats. The judge denied Greene's request, pointing out that the prosecution failed to prove that Morelli's threat stood out from all the other threats Greene received. The judge noted that Greene herself admitted that getting threats was a frequent part of her political life. Threats against her, Greene told a *Washington Post* reporter, "never stop."

Source: Ruby Cramer, "The Threat: In a Time of Rising Anger, What Happened to One Man Who Threatened Rep. Marjorie Taylor Greene," *Washington Post*, April 27, 2024, retrieved at https://www.washingtonpost.com/nation/interactive/2024/marjorie-taylor-greene-threats/.

Intimacy Effect *in Gathering Places or Representative Targets*

Researchers have not fully explored the role the Intimacy Effect plays on assaults against gathering places or representative targets. It seems reasonable to speculate that those Subjects who perceive that their target somehow menaces them are more likely to carry out any threats the Subject might make. Hate crimes and racist attacks on groups or institutions fall into this category. At the very least, Subjects of Concern who target gathering places and representative targets frequently post their grievances online or by live streaming their attacks. Such postings, of course, give hardly any time for the target to respond. That, too, should be accounted for when assessing risks to such places as churches, synagogues, abortion clinics, and other entities targeted because of what they symbolize in the Subject's mind.

Chapter 5

Venues

What are the different locales in which violence takes place?
What are acts of targeted and opportunistic violence?
What is grandiosity?
What characterizes intimate partner violence?
What characterizes violence at workplaces and schools?
What characterizes violence at gathering places?
What characterizes violence against representative targets?
What characterizes violence against public figures?

What Are the Different Locales in Which Violence Takes Place?

The place and social context where targeted violence takes place – the venues – strongly influence the Subject's grievances, research and planning, and preparations. Threat managers need to assess the Subject's behaviors within the specific setting to understand the potential risks. In the following discussion, each venue is defined, its particular characteristics identified, a note of caution is given, and a short case study is presented to illustrate that particular venue. All of the case studies occurred on various college campuses across the United States. Their selection as examples was done deliberately to emphasize the point that the venue is as much a state of mind – the Subject's – as it is a geographic location. In each instance, the Subject chose a campus as the site for their violence, but the reason for acting violently differed in each situation. That place and those social contexts drove the Subject.

DOI: 10.4324/9781003543282-6

The Different Venues for Violence

Intimate partner

Schools and workplaces

Gathering places

Representative targets

Public figures

Important to Understand the Differences Among the Venues

Recognizing the differences among the different venues of violence helps pinpoint the Subject's possible motive, determine the security of that venue, and understand the nature of the relationships within that venue. These factors help gauge the potential for violence occurring within that venue. While the subject always must traverse the path to intended violence regardless of venue, the differences inherent in the various venues profoundly affect the subject's motives, degree of research, and preparations. Domestic violence differs from public figure violence, not in the process of violence, but in the subject's motive and goal. Each venue – whether it's the Subject's workplace, a gathering place, or a representative target – has its own unique characteristics. These provide different perspectives on the risk of violence.

More About
Venues and the Subject's Path to Intended Violence

Subjects intending an act of violence must navigate the path to intended violence, but the differences inherent in the various venues profoundly affect the Subject's motive, target knowledge, target accessibility to the Subject, and exposure to attack. In all events, the venue is determined by the Subject's perception of their relationship to the target.

Venues Can Overlap

Venues frequently overlap. Domestic violence occurs in workplaces, at churches, and other places the Subject knows the target will likely be. Synagogues and churches, although clearly gathering places, may also represent something offensive to the Subject's prejudices. Threat managers need to determine the attraction the target or target location holds for the Subject, *from the Subject's point of view*. To prevent harm, threat managers need to understand why the Subject might be drawn to a specific place or target.

More About
Venue

Knowing the venue from the Subject's point of view provides the threat manager great insight into the Subject's intent, motive, and ability to commit a violent act. Venue places in context the Subject's relationship to the target, what they know about the target's personal affairs, and the Subject's ability to reach the target.

What Are Acts of Targeted and Opportunistic Violence?

Subjects who engage in targeted violence focus their attack on specific individuals. Those who engage in opportunistic violence aim their attack at whoever happens to be at the location where the Subject launches their assault. In opportunistic violence, the Subject does not care who the specific victims are. Instead, the Subject targets the locations, either because they know people will be there or because the location itself represents something offensive to the Subject. Opportunistic violence often results in multiple injuries and fatalities, especially since the Subject may measure the success of their assault by a large body count. Subjects may also combine targeted and opportunistic violence in one assault. They go to a place looking for their former intimate partner or the supervisor who disciplined them, for example, but use that opportunity to attack the partner or supervisor plus anyone else who happens to be there.

More About
Targeted and Opportunistic Violence

Subjects of Concern engaging in targeted violence direct their attacks at specific individuals.

Subjects of Concern using opportunistic violence act randomly, attacking anyone who happens to be at the site of the violence.

What Is Grandiosity?

Violence frequently contains elements of the Subject's grandiosity, of making their grievance bigger than themselves or the people they attack. Synagogues, reproductive health care facilities, church denominations such as mosques, and Black Lives Matter events, among countless others, suffer this type of crusading violence simply because of what they represent to the Subject or due to the demographics of the people at the location. Getting a large body count seems to enhance the notoriety the Subject seeks. These acts often stem from inflated egos, as though the Subject wants to show that their life equals the lives of many others combined. The Subject often disguises that motivation by wrapping the violent act in the mantle of some larger, greater cause.

What Characterizes Intimate Partner Violence?

Several factors distinguish intimate partner violence from targets in other venues. Threats, for example, do serve as good indicators of future violence, especially when the threats fail to control the partner's behavior. While the threats work, that is, by intimidating the target enough to do the Subject's bidding, the Subject has no need to carry out the threat. Calling the Subject's bluff, however, strongly induces the Subject to carry out the threat.

Venue Characteristics for Intimate Partner Violence

Threats of violence are good indicators of future violence.

If threats prove effective at changing or controlling the target's behavior, the Subject may not need to resort to violence.

Due to prior knowledge about the target, the Subject needs to conduct little overt research.

Risk of violence moves to the target's location.

Target's behavior can challenge intervention strategies by siding with the Subject.

Violence centers on issues of control and dominance.

Leaving the relationship does not lessen the risk and may increase it.

Access to firearms increases the risk of using them while lessening the need for preparation.

Less Need for Research

Intimacy relieves the Subject from conducting overt research on the target since they already know so much about the target's habits and routines. The risk of violence also moves to the target's location because the Subject knows where the target lives, works, worships, and socializes. That knowledge makes it easier for the Subject to choose a location that suits their plans for the attack. Unfortunately, current or previous intimate relationships may also lead the target to behave in ways that raise the risk to them, thus complicating any management strategy implemented by the threat manager. The target may taunt the Subject, further increasing their ire, or the target may ultimately side with the Subject against the threat manager's efforts to manage the Subject.

Control and Dominance

In most cases of intimate partner violence, the Subject's intent comes from demanding control and dominance over the partner or former partner. As a result, even if the partner leaves or otherwise ends the relationship, the risk of harm does not necessarily decrease.

The Case of the
Jealous Husband
Intimate Partner Violence on College Campus

Brandon Morrissette accused his wife of having an affair with R.J. Long, a mutual friend of the couple. On Monday, April 23, 2023, Morrissette waited for his wife and Long outside the Humanities Building at Rose

State College in Midwest City, Oklahoma. Morrissette no doubt knew that his wife and Long took a course together in that building. He made sure he arrived outside the building at the end of the class. When his wife and Long emerged together from the building, Morrissette confronted them and then shot Long, who died at the scene. Morrissette then surrendered to the police.

Source: Shelby Montgomery, "Suspect Accused in Deadly Rose State College Shooting Thought Wife Was Having Affair, Court Docs Say," KOCO News 5, April 25, 2023, reviewed at https://www.koco.com/article/oklahoma-midwest-city-rose-state-college-shooting-court-documents/43695524.

What Characterizes Violence at Workplaces and Schools?

Violence at workplaces or schools often results from personal conflicts. Workers may feel slighted by not getting promoted or insulted by disciplinary actions taken against them. Students may feel picked upon or teased by their peers or aggrieved by some actions of their teachers or school staff.

Venue Characteristics for School/Workplace Violence

Workplace and school violence are often personal, with the Subject seeking revenge for particular grievances.

Leakage, that is, telling others of the Subject's plans, occurs frequently.

School/workplace violence often combines targeted and opportunistic violence.

Intimate partner violence frequently spills into the workplace because the Subject knows where the target works, their routines, and their lifestyle.

The most common motive is the search for personalized justice taking the form of revenge.

The Case of the
Unhappy Graduate Student
Workplace Violence on College Campus

On August 28, 2023, Tailei Qi, a graduate student at the University of North Carolina at Chapel Hill killed his mentor, Zijie Yan, an associate professor in the Applied Physical Sciences Department. Qi worked in Yan's research group and co-authored two research papers with the professor. Qi found the professor working in the lab where they conducted their research. After shooting Yan, Qi left the building. Police arrested him an hour and a half after the shooting.

Source: Michael Levenson, "U.N.C. Graduate Student Is Charged in Fatal Shooting of Professor," *New York Times,* August 29, 2023, reviewed at https://www.nytimes.com/2023/08/29/us/unc-chapel-hill-shooting-gunman-charges.html?searchResultPosition=14.

What Characterizes Violence at Gathering Places?

Places where people gather, for whatever reason, attract some violent Subjects simply because the Subject knows people will be there. Churches, schools, sporting events, shopping malls, and any other places people go to provide the setting for this type of violence. These Subjects seem less interested in who they assault so long as it is someone, preferably many people. They usually intend for their acts of violence to make a statement about some perceived grievance, engage in grandiosity by making their petty complaints into something larger, or gain notoriety.

Acts of Egotism

Violence at places people gather often involves acts of egotism. It's as if the subject needs to prove that their life is worth the lives of many other people. This egotism declares that the injury done to the Subject demands the sacrifice of many others in retribution. The randomness of the target selection – basically targets of opportunity – characterizes violence at gathering places.

Venue Characteristics for Gathering Place Violence

Combines targeted and opportunistic violence.
  Subject desires notoriety or infamy based on large body count.
  Subject claims association with cause or seeks to connect to a well-known location or event.

The Case of the
Grandiose Shooter
Gathering Place Violence on College Campus

On the evening of February 13, 2023, Anthony McRae took a bus to the campus of Michigan State University. McRae had no association with the college, neither as a student or an employee. Once on campus, he entered Berkey Hall. A class was in progress in Room 114. McRae fired repeatedly into the classroom, hitting seven students, two fatally. McRae then went to the campus student union, "a popular place for students to eat and study," and killed a third student. Hours later, when police caught up with McRae off campus, McRae fatally shot himself. He had with him two 9mm handguns, more than a dozen magazines, and 136 rounds of loose ammunition. He went to the campus looking for people gathered together, first in a classroom where a class was in session, then at the student union.

McRae also cloaked his actions in a larger, unspecified mission. Police found in McRae's possession two pages of handwritten notes dated the day before the shooting. In the notes, McRae claimed to belong to some unnamed, larger organization that had divided into teams and whose goals remained unclear. While McRae shot up MSU, he wrote, another team would be attacking Colorado Springs. A third team "will finish off the city of Lansing." By wrapping himself in such grandiosity, McRae justified his violence.

Sources: Johnny Diaz, "Michigan State to Pay $15 Million to Families of Three Slain Students," *New York Times*, December 17, 2023, reviewed at https://www.nytimes.com/2023/12/17/us/michigan-state-university-shooting-settlement.html?searchResultPosition=30; David Jesse Darcie and Moran

Dave Boucher, "Police Release Michigan State University Gunman's Note: 'Why Do People Hate Me?'" *Detroit Free Press*, March 10, 2023, reviewed at https://www.freep.com/story/news/local/michigan/2023/03/10/michigan-state-university-gunman-anthony-mcrae-note/69991547007/. See also "2023 Michigan State University Shooting," Wikipedia entry, reviewed at https://en.wikipedia.org/wiki/2023_Michigan_State_University_shooting.

What Characterizes Violence Against Representative Targets?

Certain locations become targets for violence because they represent or symbolize something to the Subject. The assault culminates in the Subject's personal crusade. These Subjects convince themselves that their cause demands a public display of violence. Lately, Subjects live stream their assaults on social media for the purpose of bringing more attention to their supposed causes.

Importance of Symbolic Value

Representative targets differ from other venues because of the symbolic value the Subject places on them. Churches, synagogues, abortion clinics, and iconic locations – like the World Trade Center towers – all hold symbolic attraction to some Subjects. Attacking them becomes a political, religious, or moral statement by the Subject denouncing or condemning whatever the symbol stands for. These Subjects do not attack individuals who have somehow offended them, they attack ideas and concepts that the location itself represents. The Subject values most the thing the target represents, not the victims.

Venue Characteristics for Representative Target Violence

Subject usually believes their cause demands public exhibition of violence.
Cause can be personal grievance or a political or religious crusade.
Combines targeted and opportunistic violence.
Subject displays grandiosity.

The Case of the
Random Shooter
Representative Target Violence on College Campus

On Friday evening, May 12, 2023, Warfield High Hawk walked south-bound along the eastern edge of Chadron State College campus in Chadron, Nebraska. As he walked, he randomly fired a rifle he had stolen. He did not appear to aim the weapon at anyone, firing into the air and at the ground. After five hours, he dropped his weapon and surrendered to police. For whatever reason, the school repre-sented something that attracted Hawk's violence.

Source: "Suspect ID'd in Chadron State College Active Shooter Investiga-tion Following Friday Arrest," KNEB 960 AM, 100.3 FM, May 13, 2023, reviewed at https://ruralradio.com/kneb-am/news/suspect-idd-in-chad-ron-state-college-active-shooter-investigation-following-friday-arrest/.

What Characterizes Violence Against Public Figures?

Subjects who target public figures do so because of the figure's public status. Politicians, high government officials, prominent business leaders, and entertainment celebrities catch the attention of both hunters and howlers because of their fame and seeming good fortune. Threat managers should keep in mind Andy Warhol's famous "15 minutes of fame" dictum. It reminds us that anyone can become famous at any time, thus transform-ing that individual into a public figure, complete with all the baggage that accompanies that status.

Consequently, public figures rarely know or even recognize their atta-ckers. The Subject may believe they have a deep emotional, even sexual, relationship with their target. As a practical matter, threat managers gain little information about the Subject from public figure targets. It also means the Subject may have little information about the target's habits and routines. Social media and the internet provide a wealth of information readily available to the Subject.

Public Figures Attract Howlers

Famous people attract more howlers than targets in other venues. Direct threats tend not to serve as useful predictors of potential violence toward these targets. Although threat managers must never discount such threats, they should also keep that finding very much in mind.

Reasons for Public Figure Pursuits

Subjects pursue public figures for a variety of reasons, but the desire to achieve infamy runs through each of the other motives. Indeed, the Subject's grievance may be that they don't have the fame and recognition the target has. Attacking the target gives them an easy way to gain attention.

Venue Characteristics for Public Figure Violence

Threats and violence derive from the target's public prominence or media personification.

Subject likely not to have personal knowledge about the target.

Subject needs to research the target to locate and gain access to the target.

Howlers make up a higher proportion of Subjects targeting public figures than in other venues.

Direct threats to public figures are poor indicators of future violence.

Predominant motive for Subject is to gain notoriety or infamy, that is, to steal the target's fame.

The Case of the
Besieged University President
Public Figure Violence on College Campus

On December 5, 2023, Claudine Gay testified before the House of Representatives Committee on Education and the Workplace. Along with the presidents of MIT and the University of Pennsylvania, Gay responded to questions regarding anti-Semitic campus demonstrations after the Israeli invasion of the Gaza Strip following the October 7 surprise attack by Hamas on Israel. "Yes, I made mistakes," Gay wrote in the *New York Times* explaining her decision to resign after only six months in office. For weeks after her testimony, she wrote, "both I and the institution to which I've devoted my professional life have been under attack ... My inbox has been flooded with invective, including death threats."

Thrust into the spotlight, Dr. Gay became a public figure and, therefore, a magnet attracting the lunatic fringe.

Source: Claudine Gay, "Claudine Gay: What Just Happened at Harvard Is Bigger Than Me," *New York Times,* January 3, 2024, reviewed at https://www.nytimes.com/2024/01/03/opinion/claudine-gay-harvard-president.html?searchResultPosition=3.

Chapter 6

Inhibitors

What are inhibitors?
What role do inhibitors play in threat management?

What Are Inhibitors?

Inhibitors consist of anything the Subject values. They can be physical possessions like homes and businesses, emotional connections with loved ones, or career and financial resources. Religious, political, and philosophical beliefs also play a significant role in shaping the Subject's actions. The Subject's health may have an impact. Perhaps most important of all, the Subject's self-esteem and sense of dignity exercise a profound influence on their behavior.

More About
What Subject's Value

What the Subject values depends entirely on what the Subject deems important. Things of value, then, are deeply personal to each individual Subject. They need not meet some rational, monetary, sentimental, or other standard of intrinsic worth. The Subject's relationship to that which they value may act like a double-edged sword, cutting both ways. That which the Subject values may inhibit the Subject from using violence because the repercussions of doing so might result in loss or harm to what they value. Conversely, the Subject may feel that they need to use violence to protect or preserve what they value. Again, that is an entirely personal choice for the Subject – and

DOI: 10.4324/9781003543282-7

one which the threat manager needs to determine based on evidence. Religion, for example, can act as a strong inhibitor, but religion can also act as a strong incentive for violence if the Subject sees themself on a religious mission like a crusade or *jihad*.

Assessing a Subject's inhibitors means determining:

1 What the Subject values.
2 What the Subject feels is necessary *to do or not do* to protect or preserve that which they value.

The Case of the *Competing Values*

Ronnie Wiggs faced a depressing dilemma. His wife, Ellen "Tippie" Wiggs needed dialysis treatments for her failing kidneys. Ronnie, 75, increasingly worried that he could not take care of her nor afford to keep paying for dialysis. Confronted by that horrific predicament, Ronnie decided he had no choice but to kill Tippie. He tried strangling her, but she woke up and told him not to do that again. He tried a second time while she underwent treatment, but she was hooked up to several monitors that got in his way. In May 2024, Tippie needed a new portal to continue the treatments. This time, Ronnie succeeded, choking her with one hand while covering her mouth and nose with his other hand to prevent her from screaming. When nurses noticed the bruising on Tippie's neck, Ronnie confessed. He told the police he killed his wife "because he could not take care of her anymore and he could not pay the medical bills."

Ronnie essentially made a choice between the things he valued.

Source: Chris Spargo, "Missouri Man Confesses to Strangling Wife in Her Hospital Because He Could Not Afford Medical Bills: Police," Inside Edition, May 7, 2024, retrieved at https://www.insideedition.com/ronnie-wiggs-missouri-murder-wife-hospital-bed-medical-bills.

Typical Inhibitors

Home

Family

Career

Financial resources

Health

Religious beliefs

Self-esteem

Reputation

Dignity

What Role Do Inhibitors Play in Threat Management?

Inhibitors and their absence act as a scale balancing an individual's positive and negative behaviors. When an individual has inhibitors, the scale tilts toward appropriate behavior. But the lack or loss of inhibitors or perceived threats to them can tip the scales toward inappropriate behavior. The power of inhibitors runs both ways: their presence leads to avoiding problematic behavior and their absence or potential loss contributes to such behavior. When evaluating inhibitors, look for quality, not just quantity. Just as importantly, the threat manager needs to pay particular attention to the recent or impending loss of any inhibitors.

Act Like Dominoes

Inhibitors act much like dominoes standing in a row. As long as each remains standing, they help shepherd the subject's behaviors toward the positive. But when one key domino topples, it risks knocking over its neighbor to set off a chain reaction that topples the remaining dominoes. Subjects falling in a downward spiral often begin losing everything important to them, including their jobs, homes, family, health, and even their grip on reality. As each fall, the controls preventing the subject from acting out violently tumble as well. Indeed, the very loss of the inhibitors acts as a strong motivation for retaliating violently.

Propping Up Inhibitors

Effective threat management recognizes the need for propping up a Subject's inhibitors whenever possible. A key strategy involves helping the Subject to resolve their grievance peacefully and legally. Cutting through bureaucratic red tape, helping resolve complicated issues, or simply offering a helping hand can play a crucial role in steering Subjects away from the path to intended violence. It can also curb problems caused by Subjects who seek attention or hope to cause disruptions.

Disinhibiting

Sometimes, organizations take actions that take away a Subject's inhibitors. Employment terminations, school expulsions, indeed, most disciplinary measures take something away from the Subject that they may treasure. This is especially true of any perceived attack on their dignity. Although such measures may be unavoidable, the threat manager needs to consciously factor in the repercussions of such disinhibiting actions in both the assessments and the selection of the best management plan. How the discipline gets handed out can have a strong effect on how the Subject perceives they are being treated. Paying special attention to the Subject's dignity and sense of self may significantly lessen the perceived hardship of the discipline. Propping up the Subject's pride and self-esteem can help defuse potentially violent reactions.

More About Inhibitors

The status of the Subject's inhibitors offers tremendous insight into the positive influences operating on the Subject. Stable inhibitors suggest a lower risk of acting violently. Weak inhibitors or, worse, inhibitors toppling due to the grievance, indicate a potential for a higher risk of violence.

Part II

The Threat Management Process

Chapter 7

Steps to an Effective Threat Management Process

What are the steps to an effective threat management process?
What is the DRA process?
What are criteria for reporting?
Is the process continuous?

What Are the Steps to an Effective Threat Management Process?

Stepping toward an effective threat management process requires:

1 Recognizing the need for a threat management program tailored to your organization's unique challenges.
2 Choosing and training a designated receiver to act as threat manager overseeing the entire threat management process.
3 Defining specific behavioral criteria that need to be reported to the designated threat manager.
4 Training all members of the organization in the reporting criteria and how to report incidents to the threat manager.
5 Identifying subject matter experts (e.g., human resource specialists, attorneys, and security managers) that the threat manager can consult.
6 Establishing a system to Detect, Report, and Act (DRA) on inappropriate behaviors.

Figure 7.1 illustrates the steps for setting up an effective threat management process.

DOI: 10.4324/9781003543282-9

Process for Handling Reportable Behaviors

Step 1	Step 2	Step 3
Designated Receiver Identified, Assigned Program Responsibility, Establishes Points of Contact	Designated Receiver Defines and Disseminates Reporting Criteria	Designated Receiver Trains Personnel on Reporting Criteria and Reporting Process

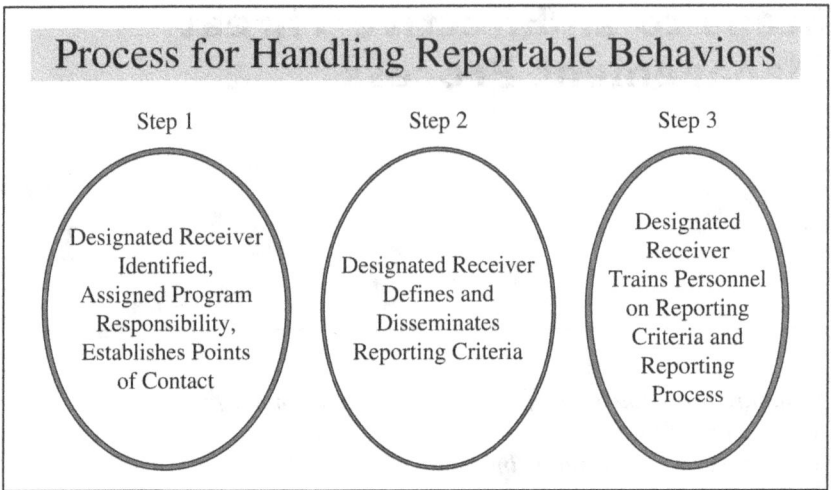

Figure 7.1 Process for Detecting Reportable Behaviors

What Is the *DRA* Process?

Following the *DRA* process helps identify potential problem individuals early on. The process consists of:

- *Detecting (D)*: Appoint designated receivers trained in threat management fundamentals who then can train everyone within the organization on what, how, and where to report inappropriate behaviors they may witness.
- *Reporting (R)*: Establish clear lines of communication for individuals witnessing reportable behaviors to report those behaviors to the designated threat manager.
- *Acting (A)*: The threat manager initiates the threat management process by receiving reports, confirming a potential problem, responding to emergencies, and moving on to the assessment and management stages of the threat management process.

Figure 7.2 shows how the DRA process fits within an effective threat management approach.

DRA Within Threat Management Process

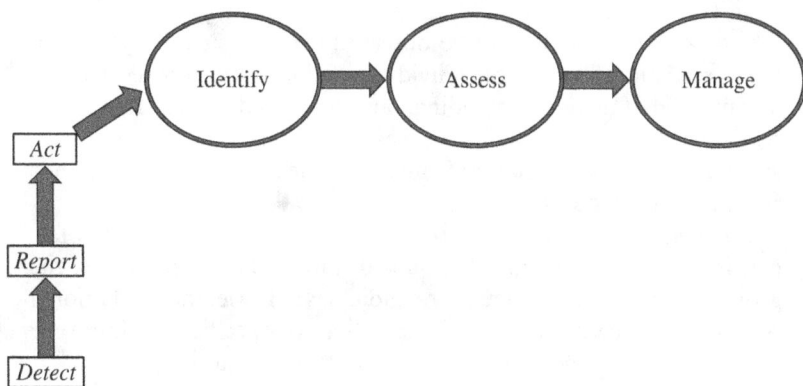

Figure 7.2 The *DRA* Process Within an Effective Threat Management Approach

What Are Criteria for Reporting?

Criteria for reporting should be broad enough to capture various problem behaviors. The "All Threat – All Target Reporting Criteria" broadside below offers a universal reporting criteria model. The broadside organizes the criteria along the path to intended violence. Clearly defined criteria offer several advantages.

1 Provides a reasonable, defensible threshold for what behaviors will prompt a report and subsequent action.
2 Clarifies the problematic behaviors that need reporting, thus avoiding confusion and misunderstandings.
3 Eliminates subjective biases of the witness.
4 Makes it more difficult for someone observing the behavior to avoid getting involved.
5 Prevents minimizing or dismissing problem behaviors.

Below are sample reporting criteria that can be used as a basis for customizing within your organization.

All Threat – All Target Reporting Criteria

The following criteria apply to observed behaviors or reported contacts from an individual or individuals acting in concert received by any method of delivery, including, but not limited to, verbal, written, telephone, fax, text, e-mail, all types of social media, Instagram, instant messaging, information from a credible informant, or obtained from diaries, videos, or audio recordings.

The criteria apply when the behaviors or contacts concern any target, including an individual; groups of individuals identified by the group's association, sex, race, religion, sexual orientation, national origin, family connection, social standing, or specific location; type of locale, geographic region, or the general public at large.

Report all threats of physical harm made by any method, whether direct, veiled, or conditional, concerning any target. Threats may also be nonverbal or implied by behavior or pattern of conduct.

Indicators of Grievance

Any extraordinarily problematic terminations, suspensions, expulsions, disciplinary measures, or denial of service, preferably prior to final implementation by the organization against the subject.

References to hallucinations, including receiving direct communications or orders.

Irrational or unreasonable demands, solicitations, or claims of being owed something by the target.

Obsessive admiration or affection for the target or efforts to contact or control the target.

Inappropriate or suspicious expression of personal loss, injustice, or desire for revenge.

Information about potentially violent domestic or personal dispute, in particular the issuance of a protective or restraining order.

Indicators of Ideation

Inappropriate display of, or references to, weapons or any other method of inflicting harm.

Inappropriate or disturbing references to, or identification with, death, violence, mass killing, violence in the media, or specific previous violent acts or actors.

Expression of irrational or delusional beliefs, particularly containing violent or paranoid themes.

Threats of physical harm made by any method, whether direct, veiled, or conditional, concerning any target.

Nonverbal threats or threats implied by behavior or pattern of conduct.

Any references to, or failed attempts at, suicide or self-harm.

Expressions of hopelessness or belief that the subject has no alternatives to violence.

Indicators of Research and Planning

Any suspicious activity, such as surveillance, suspicious inquiries, unusual interest in the target, or any other untoward attention toward the target.

Obsessive interest in the target, including stalking, research, or unusual knowledge or specific information on a person, group, or locale.

Indicators of Preparation

Evidence of final act behaviors such as preparing a will, disposing of property, saying goodbye, last rites, fasting, cleansing, confessing, or justifying the threatened act of violence.

Obtaining or preparing weapons, armaments, military-style clothing, methods, and attire inspired by prior violent acts, or other well-publicized attack-related materials.

Rehearsing, practicing, or communicating plans and objectives.

Recognizing approaching symbolic dates or events.

Indicators of Breach

Verbal or physical abuse, including assault, attempted assault, vandalism, or violent or threatening gestures.

Aggressive or emotional outbursts directed toward a person, group, location, or inanimate objects.

Testing or probing security perimeters or systems.

In addition to the above, report any questionable, untoward, sinister, or otherwise suspect behaviors or contacts.

Is the Process Continuous?

For every reported incident, threat managers must continue gathering facts, reassessing the evolving situation, and applying new strategies based on new assessments. New information feeds fresh assessment, leading to the refinement of the management strategies, then around again. This iterative approach makes sure that the process remains dynamic and responsive to emerging threats.

Chapter 8

Identifying

What will happen once the DRA process is in effect?
What is fact-finding?
How does a focused inquiry differ from a basic approach?
What are the "need-to-knows" and what do they mean?
What are the knowns and unknowns in any given situation?
How important is taking situational context into consideration?

What Will Happen Once the DRA Process Is in Effect?

Once the threat manager stands up the DRA process, members of the organization will start reporting inappropriate behaviors they witness. With a proper reporting procedure in place, the threat manager can then begin screening these reports, triaging, and filtering out the mistakes and overblown incidents. All of that requires immediate and accurate fact-finding, both as an initial screening and as an ongoing effort to inform accurate assessments.

What Is Fact-Finding?

Effective threat management relies on constantly gathering information, evaluating its meaning within the current situation, and responding to new or changing situations. Ask questions like:

- Who did what to whom?
- What motivates the Subject?
- Why did they choose that particular target?
- In effect: What is going on?

Fact-Finding

"Fact-finding" involves collecting and analyzing relevant information. The threat manager keeps collecting facts, assessing their importance, and responding as needed for as long as the Subject remains a risk.

DOI: 10.4324/9781003543282-10

Basic Rules for Fact-Finding

In collecting the information, follow these basic rules.

1. Be objective, thorough, and comprehensive.
2. Determine the who, what, where, when, and why of the situation.
3. Prefer direct sources over unverified content, rumors, and gossip.
4. Ask and answer appropriate follow-up questions.
5. Evaluate the credibility and biases of everyone providing information.
6. Record all the information.

How Does a Focused Inquiry Differ From a Basic Approach?

Basically, threat assessments evaluate something that *happened* to determine the risk of some future violent act. The key to making this determination lies in distinguishing between what is known and what is unknown at any given time. Doing so requires going beyond a basic or traditional fact-finding approach by using a focused, in-depth inquiry.

Table 8.1 compares this in-depth approach with more basic fact-finding methods.

As the right column indicates, effective fact-finding digs deeper than getting surface-level answers. In gathering information, the threat manager should always ask not only what happened, but why it happened and under what circumstances. Digging deeper offers the best insights into the Subject's intent, motive, and ability.

Table 8.1 Basic Fact-Finding Approach Versus Focused Inquiry

Basic fact-finding approach	Focused inquiry
What did the Subject say or do?	What about the situation relates to the Subject's choice of context, including the circumstances of the situation and the content of any communication?
Does the Subject have a criminal history?	Has the Subject engaged in violence in the past? Is the Subject indicating thoughts of violence currently? Is the Subject behaving as if violence is the only resolution to their grievance?
Does the Subject have a firearm?	Does the Subject possess or have access to violent means? Does the Subject show fascination with violent acts of any type? Is the Subject currently seeking to obtain a weapon or the means to carry out a violent act?

What Are the "Need-to-Knows" and What Do They Mean?

Effective threat management requires addressing at least 20 basic questions to get a thorough understanding of any situation. Used correctly, these "need-to-knows" provide a detailed and focused method of gathering facts. They explore the circumstances and context of any situation. Keeping the need-to-knows in mind helps the threat manager keep track of the facts currently known and the questions still unanswered or only partially answered. Asking the questions – not all can always be answered – helps uncover what the Subject said or did, but also why they did it and what they might be planning. Table 8.2 lists the 20 need-to-knows and explains what to look for in answering each question and what the answers potentially reveal.

Table 8.2 Need-to-Knows Explained

Need-to-know question	What to look for	What question reveals
1. How did the Subject choose to approach the target?	In writing Distant communication Face-to-face communication Third-party informing Suspicious activity	Insight into intent, motive, and ability. How the Subject chooses to approach the target tells a lot about the Subject's willingness to expose themselves, their determination, and their current ability to get near the target.
2. What about the situation indicates the Subject's identity and physical proximity to the target; in other words, who and where is the Subject?	Identified or anonymous Current proximity to target	Current relationship and physical proximity between Subject and target.
3. What about the situation indicates who or what the Subject is targeting; in other words, who or what is the target?	Precise or vague Practical or symbolic Person or place	Determine who or what the Subject is currently targeting.
4. What about the situation indicates the type of venue being targeted and what is it about the venue that gives insight into the Subject's intent, motive, and ability?	Intimate partner School/workplace Gathering place Representative target Public figure	Determines context for assessing the situation and gives insight into the Subject's motive and ability. Helps clarify the Subject's relation to the target.

(Continued)

Table 8.2 (Continued)

Need-to-know question	What to look for	What question reveals
5. What is the relationship between the Subject and the target in terms of the *Intimacy Effect*?	Relationship, real or imagined by Subject, between Subject and target.	Insight into the chemistry between Subject and target. The *Intimacy Effect* can help assess any threats made by the Subject.
6. What about the situation relates to the Subject's choice of context, including the circumstances and content?	The Subject chose how to approach.	Insight into the Subject's choices and their intent, motive, and ability.
7. Is the target currently accessible to the Subject?	Where at this time are Subject and target in relation to each other?	Insight into the current state of the situation.
8. Does the Subject have the ability and motivation to take advantage of any current accessibility to the target?	Determine the Subject's current capability for violence.	Snapshot of where Subject is currently and what Subject is doing.
9. Is there a known history of previous contacts with the target or other targets by this Subject?	Determine the Subject's criminal history, medical issues, threat manager's database of previous incidents, and target knowledge.	Insight into the Subject's previous demeanor, capability, and past behaviors. Past behavior is suggestive of future behavior.
10. Does the Subject have a history of violence or threatening behaviors, including any criminal behavior?	Determine the Subject's criminal history, medical issues, threat manager's database of previous incidents, target knowledge, and neighbors' and colleagues' experiences dealing with the Subject.	Insight into the Subject's previous demeanor, capability, and past behaviors. Past behavior is suggestive of future behavior.
11. What is the Subject's knowledge about the target's current situation?	Level of research or prior knowledge about the target by Subject. What does the venue indicate?	Indicates the degree of the Subject's knowledge – or lack thereof – about the target.

(Continued)

Table 8.2 (Continued)

Need-to-know question	What to look for	What question reveals
12. Is the Subject seeking knowledge about the target and the target's current situation?	Target research critical step on the path to intended violence. What does the venue indicate? What information is available on the internet?	Measure how actively or energetically the Subject seeks information.
13. Does the Subject's behavior indicate mental health issues, including suicidality?	Positive indicators of the Subject's current mental health. History of mental health issues.	Insight into Subject's current mental condition and state of mind. Focus on how functional Subject is, i.e. is Subject capable of violence?
14. Does the Subject possess, have access to, or give evidence of a fascination with weaponry of any type?	Area of inquiry beyond asking if the Subject owns a firearm. Focus on any kind of weapon.	Preparation is a critical step on the path to intended violence.
15. Is the Subject currently seeking to obtain a weapon?	Evidence of preparation.	Preparation is a critical step on the path to intended violence.
16. What is the status of the Subject's inhibitors, including any recent losses?	Indicators of influences – positive or negative – on Subject. What does Subject value?	Indicates stability or instability of the Subject's current situation.
17. Has the Subject exhibited controlling, isolating, or jealous behaviors toward the target?	Evidence of the need to dominate others in a particular social environment.	Evidence of how the Subject perceives their current relationship to target.
18. Does the Subject have a history of, or is currently, abusing alcohol, drugs, or prescription medicines?	Check criminal history, medical history, and information from neighbors and colleagues.	Can Subject control their behavior?

(Continued)

Table 8.2 (Continued)

Need-to-know question	What to look for	What question reveals
19. Does the Subject have any relevant medical issues?	Check criminal history, medical history, information from neighbors and colleagues, and Subject's behaviors.	Determines physical state of Subject and their ability to carry out violence.
20. Has the Subject engaged in any final act behaviors?	Actions indicating the Subject expects to die soon.	Subject's current expectations for the future.

More About
How the Need-to-Knows Inform the Threat Management Process

Threat managers should:

- Focus on what the Subject did to gain attention. That helps to identify.
- Determine the knowns and the unknowns of each situation. That helps to assess.
- Concentrate on the Subject's inappropriate behaviors and the circumstances in which those behaviors occurred. That helps to manage.

What Are the Knowns and Unknowns in Any Given Situation?

Since threat assessments always evaluate something that happened, the threat manager always knows certain facts, otherwise they would have nothing to assess. At the same time, threat managers need to keep in mind all the unknowns about the situation at any given time. What the threat manager knows and doesn't know varies from case to case. Using the need-to-knows helps keep track of what is known and unknown at any given time.

How Important Is Taking Situational Context into Consideration?

The need-to-knows play a crucial role in all three stages of the threat management process. In using the need-to-knows, weigh each question within the circumstances of the situation. Each question's importance varies depending on what's going on. For example, on its face possessing a firearm would automatically raise the risk posed by the Subject, but that information's value diminishes in the context of finding out the Subject only has an old inherited shotgun and dislikes guns. Mental health concerns might seem significant until information surfaces proving the Subject sought and continues to receive appropriate treatment. Finding such things out requires keeping an open mind and asking detailed, in-depth questions.

More About
What Threat Managers Need to Know
About the Need-to-Knows

Not all need-to-knows are equal. Some carry far more weight than others. The importance of each question needs to be weighed within the context of each situation.

Low-risk assessments usually require knowing more about the situation than high-risk assessments. High-risk situations tend to be obvious, their degree of risk apparent and immediate. Low-risk situations need more confirmation and more evidence that the Subject does not intend violence. They sometimes require, if not proving, at least substantiating a negative.

Chapter 9

Assessing

What needs assessing?
How often should I reassess the situation?
What are the "always-knowns?"
How do I use the path to intended violence to assess the situation?
Has the Subject acted like a howler?
What is the impact of the venue on any given situation?
What is the impact of how the Subject perceives the target?
How do I factor in the Intimacy Effect?
How do I recognize good news?
Why do I need to avoid playing the "What If?" Game?
What is the best antidote to the "What If?" Game?
What is the best way to communicate a threat assessment?
What is the best format for a written threat assessment?

What Needs Assessing?

Threat assessments evaluate something that happened. Ideally, someone trained on the reporting criteria notices some inappropriate behavior and reports the incident to the designated receiver. Because something occurred, the threat assessor can always deal with facts known to have taken place based on the initial reports. Effective threat assessments require approaching the situation thoughtfully, without preconceptions, and sticking strictly to what happened. Facts, and facts alone, feed assessments.

How Often Should I Reassess the Situation?

For any situation, something is always known to support initial assessments. As the situation develops and the threat manager continues

DOI: 10.4324/9781003543282-11

their fact-finding, new facts emerge. These require reassessments and adjustments to the threat management response. Assessments are frozen in time with very short shelf lives. The threat assessor must consider fresh information, whether from the need-to-knows or the Subject's recent actions, to maintain an up-to-date, informed analysis of the facts. Threat assessments continually analyze an individual's behavior to gauge how close they might be to committing a violent act or causing further disruption.

What Are the "Always-Knowns?"

Each assessment must be seen as a single snapshot in time with a very short shelf life. The best assessors simply think through what is known and unknown about any situation to determine the Subject's direction on the path to intended violence. Since the threat assessor's attention focuses on a reported event, the assessor always knows *something*. That something supports the initial assessments. These "Always-Knowns" vary from case to case, but the initial and subsequent reports always give the threat assessor something known. The two examples below illustrate how much can be deduced from even bare-bones reports.

Always-Knowns – Example 1

The Facts

Target receives a voicemail on the office telephone stating, "I'm going to kill you." Time stamp indicates the call was received at 2:00 a.m. that morning. Target reports they do not recognize the voice. Target knows of no reason why anyone would leave such a message.

The Knowns at This Time

1 Subject chose to telephone rather than write or approach.
2 Subject chose to call when the target was likely not in the office.
3 Subject chose to remain anonymous.
4 Target cannot identify any likely suspects.

Always-Knowns – Example 2

The Facts

Two television stations receive telephone calls. The caller identifies himself as "Grandson of Sam." States "there is a contract out on" a local assistant district attorney. Concluded with the statement, "He will be eliminated. I rode alone with him in the elevator yesterday at 10:00 a.m." The assistant district attorney confirmed another man was in the elevator at about that time.

The Knowns at This Time

1   Subject chose to physically approach the target.
2   Subject chose to reveal that approach by calling the television stations.
3   Subject intended to frighten the target after the fact.
4   Subject seeking publicity by calling the television stations.
5   Subject identifies with famous mass murderer.

How Do I Use the Path to Intended Violence to Assess the Situation?

Effective threat assessment first requires the threat assessor to look for any behavior indicative of movement along the path to intended violence. Recognizing those behaviors is crucial for understanding and evaluating any potential threat posed by the Subject. The threat manager should determine if the reported situation provides answers to any of the following questions:

- Has the Subject expressed a grievance or sense of injustice?
- Does the Subject state or hint at violent thoughts or a desire to avenge a wrong?
- Has the Subject conducted any research on the target?
- Does the Subject's behavior resemble that of someone following a plan?
- Is the Subject making any preparations to commit a violent act?
- Has the Subject approached the target?

These questions help evaluate the Subject's known behaviors. Answering them provides valuable insights into the Subject's possible intentions.

Has the Subject Acted Like a Howler?

The threat assessor should also explore if the reported situation gives any suggestion of howler-like behaviors by the Subject.

Looking at the situation from this angle helps understand whether or not the Subject engaged in behaviors typical of someone seeking attention or trying to create disruptions rather than planning or intending a violent attack.

What Is the Impact of the Venue on Any Given Situation?

Does anything about the reported situation suggest the type of venue in which the Subject perceives themselves to be? The threat assessor should take care to analyze this from the Subject's point of view, even if it doesn't align with reality. For example, the Subject may suffer a delusion that they have a romantic or sexual relationship with the target. Having some idea of the perceived venue will give the threat assessor a better handle for determining the value of any specific threats and the motives underlying the Subject's behaviors.

What Is the Impact of How the Subject Perceives the Target?

Threat assessments vary significantly depending on how the Subject perceives the target. Subjects threatening someone they see as a public figure reach radically different conclusions from threat assessments on Subjects focusing on current or former intimate partners. The credibility of any explicit threats differs dramatically between the two situations. Assessments made in the context of a workplace or school also differ from other venues, as do those regarding gathering places or representative targets.

More About
Determining Target Venue

In determining the target venue, it only matters how the Subject perceives their relationship to the target.

How Do I Factor in the *Intimacy Effect?*

Determining the Subject's venue allows the threat assessor to use the *Intimacy Effect*. This helps gauge the value of any threats made by the Subject. The more intimate or interpersonal the Subject sees their relationship with the target, the higher the risk of the Subject carrying out threats of violence, especially if the threats fail to control the target's behavior. The nature of the perceived relationship influences the potential severity of the threat.

More About
Assessing the Value of Threats

In assessing the value of threats in interpersonal relationships, always measure the effectiveness of the threat in controlling the target's behavior. Targets who do as the threat demands are less likely to suffer the promise of the threat than those targets who defy or ignore the threat. In sum, if the threat works, the Subject has no need to actually carry it out.

How Do I Recognize Good News?

Too often, threat assessors have trouble accepting good news. It sometimes takes a conscious effort to recognize when the Subject's behavior has changed direction for the better. Disgruntled former employees may forgo their complaints against their former employer once they get a new job. Disappointed lovers may get over their frustrations after finding a new

More About
Accepting Good News

Assessments must include any positives:

- Presence of inhibitors.
- Positive behavior changes.
- Life improvements.
- Change in Subject's focus away from target.

intimate partner. Delusional Subjects may respond well to mental health therapies. Threat assessors must avoid becoming so jaded that they can't recognize positive changes as they occur. They need to keep an open mind when assessing evolving situations.

Why Do I Need to Avoid Playing the "What If?" Game?

Targets, especially, fall prey to playing the "What If?" Game, a temptation threat assessors should studiously avoid. This game essentially involves letting one's imagination conjure up various scenarios that, while not currently occurring, could potentially develop. The game relies on conjectures divorced from the actual facts. It takes the form of asking those questions the answers to which can only be dire. What if the Subject buys a gun? What do I do if the Subject shows up at my home? What if the Subject goes after my family? What if the Subject is building a bomb? What if the Subject flies an airplane into my house? Any questions that focus on worst-case scenarios tend to lead to unnecessary anxiety or fear. Threat managers must stick to the known facts and avoid speculative thinking.

What Is the Best Antidote to the "What If?" Game?

Facts remain the best antidote to the temptations of the "What If?" Game. By assessing only the known, the threat assessor grounds their assessments in the reality of the situation and not in the infinite universe of what might be. Stick to the facts. That means:

- Include any positive information.
- Avoid conjectures and speculations.
- At all costs, never engage in asking "What If?" questions.

More About
Effective Threat Assessments

- Assess the always-knowns, using them to aid in identifying the unknowns.
- Stick to the facts.
- Determine the venue from the Subject's point of view.
- Locate the Subject's behaviors along the path to intended violence.
- Compare the Subject's behaviors to how hunters and howlers behave.

What Is the Best Way to Communicate a Threat Assessment?

Threat assessments are best communicated in writing. Written assessments freeze the analysis in time and place, avoid confusion by establishing a record, and, by following a specific format, help focus the threat assessor on the facts. Conversely, oral assessments risk being misinterpreted. They rely too much on memory, both the threat assessor's and the individual who hears the assessment. By making the assessment in writing, the threat assessor can lay out all the facts they have at that time, thus helping bring the situation under assessment into sharper focus. It also then creates a record for future referrals. As new facts emerge, the threat assessor can revise the assessment, updating the situation and further honing the analysis. Although writing out the assessment may take up valuable time that could be used in managing the situation, threat managers will find that taking that time – except in emergencies – is worth the effort. Emergencies are self-evident and require immediate responses, not well-thought-out analyses. The situations that require assessment are those where the degree of risk is not so readily apparent and, therefore, not urgent so much as in need of deliberate and considered analysis of the facts.

What Is the Best Format for a Written Threat Assessment?

The best format for a written threat assessment consists of answering four basic questions. The questions allow the threat manager to think through the situation methodically and comprehensively. Answering the questions highlights what is known about the situation *at this time*, what the assessor makes of the situation currently, the assessor's suggested protective response, and what management strategy seems best suited to the situation at present.

What Is Known About the Situation at This Time?

The threat assessment should provide a concise synopsis of the known facts without adornment or using unnecessary adjectives and adverbs. It should include the reason prompting the assessment, such as a threat, suspicious activity, or some other inappropriate communication that fell within the organization's reporting criteria. The answer should also include any unknowns at the time of the assessment to help measure the validity or credibility of the assessment. Pointing out the unknowns helps guide what additional information is needed and in what priority, thereby providing a guide for continued fact-finding. It also highlights any gaps in the current assessment. Future assessments can then be compared to previous ones to make sure that new facts are included in new assessments.

What Is the Assessment of the Known Facts at This Time?

The assessment should take into account *all* of the facts known at the time of the assessment. It should incorporate the method of delivery of the inappropriate communication or contact, weigh the influence of any inhibitors in the Subject's life, and determine if the *Intimacy Effect* is at play. The assessor should also spell out the facts supporting their assessment. Most crucially, the assessment should be based solely on the facts known at the time of the assessment and should absolutely avoid making any conjectures. In addition, the assessment should balance the knowns against the unknowns and recognize which factors in the present situation carry more weight than other factors. In addition to accounting for the circumstances prompting the assessment, the threat assessor should also examine the context of the situation. That involves looking for evidence of significant changes in the Subject's life or living arrangements. All of these influences – or absence of them – should be spelled out in the assessment. Each assessment should include the prepositional phrase "at this time" in order to freeze the assessment to that particular moment with those known facts.

What Is the Recommended Protective Response?

Receiving an inappropriate communication or contact can be an unnerving experience for anyone. It may signal some impending peril for the target and the target's family. As a result, threat management involves managing not only the Subject but the potential target as well. Consequently, the threat manager should always recommend a protective response even if it is simply providing the target with a personal security briefing to remind them to maintain situational awareness and to immediately report to the threat manager anything suspicious or disconcerting. The protective response should always be directly proportionate to the level of risk assessed in the threat assessment. Just as important, the justification for the response should be clearly defined so that in the future the response can be scaled back as the situation improves or the threat management strategy succeeds. Leaving the protective response open-ended allows the target to object at any lowering of the protection.

What Are the Recommended Threat Management Strategies?

The level of risk identified in the current threat assessment dictates the most appropriate threat management strategy in each situation. The strategies are defined below, ranging from least to most confrontational. Their selection, however, should not be done in any kind of order. The threat manager should select the most appropriate or effective strategy customized to the current situation and current assessed risk. The strategy should be proportionate to the risk. The threat manager should apply each strategy flexibly with the full awareness that once they implement a strategy, the nature of the situation changes. This requires reassessing the situation with the possibility of replacing or fine-tuning the management strategies.

Sample Written Threat Assessment – Example 1
Threatening Statement on Office Voice Mail

Message Left June 3, 20__ @ 2:00 a.m.

1 **The facts**: Unknown Subject left a voice mail on target's office telephone stating, "I'm going to kill you." Voice mail time stamp noted receiving the call at 2:00 a.m. The target maintains regular business hours and would be known not to be in the office at that time. The target states they do not recognize the voice and do not know of anyone who would have a reason to leave such a message.

2 **Threat assessment**: The situation is assessed as low risk *at this time*. The Subject chose to telephone, thus keeping a physical distance between themselves and their target. The Subject chose to place the call when the target would likely not be available to receive it, thus increasing the chance of being able to leave a message. The Subject chose to remain anonymous. Subject's message intended to frighten the target with no evidence Subject was in a position to act on the threat at this time.

3 **Protective response**: Target should be given a personal security briefing reminding them to maintain situational awareness. Target should be advised to call 911 if they notice any suspicious or concerning events, after which they should immediately notify this office. Target should be assured that this office will continue to monitor the situation and will immediately assess and respond to any new activity on the part of the Subject.

4 **Threat management strategy**: At this time, the most appropriate strategy is to employ a passive watch-and-wait approach to monitor future events and respond appropriately. If the Subject is not heard from again after two weeks, this office will reassess the situation. If new incidents occur, this office will immediately assess the risk and implement the most effective protective response and threat management strategy.

Sample Written Threat Assessment – Example 2
Suspicious Incident

June 3, 20__ @ 10:00 a.m.

1 **The facts**: Unknown Subject telephoned two local television stations identifying themselves as "Grandson of Sam," a possible reference to a serial killer in New York City in 1976. The subject stated over the telephone to individuals at both television stations that "there is a contract out on" the local assistant district attorney. The subject further stated, "He will be eliminated. I rode alone with the ADA yesterday at 10:00 a.m." ADA confirmed a lone man rode in the elevator with the ADA at about that time the day before.

2 **Threat assessment**: The situation is assessed as high risk *at this time*. The Subject chose to physically approach the target by riding alone in the elevator with the ADA, thereby showing his ability to access the target. The subject chose to reveal that approach by reporting it to two local television stations, thereby increasing the chance of publicizing the event. By reporting it, the Subject intended to frighten the target after the incident. The subject's reference to an infamous serial killer shows they identify with the killer.

3 **Protective response**: Target should be given a personal security briefing and should be provided an escort while in the building and to and from their personal vehicle. Target should be advised to call 911 if they notice any suspicious or concerning events, after which they should immediately notify this office. Target should be assured that this office will continue to monitor the situation and will immediately assess and respond to any new activity on the part of the Subject.

4 **Threat management strategy**: At this time, the most appropriate strategy is to employ an active watch and wait approach to try to identify and locate the Subject while increasing security around the target. Security should be in position to immediately respond to future suspicious activities directed at the target. If the Subject approaches the target again, they should be immediately detained until an arrest warrant can be obtained. If the Subject is identified, this office will immediately assess the risk, implement the most effective protective response, and seek the Subject's arrest and incarceration. If the Subject is not heard from again after a reasonable time, this office will reassess the situation taking that silence into account.

Chapter 10

Managing

How do I determine the intervention goal?
What are the various intervention approaches?
What are the nonconfrontational strategies?
What are the considerations in interviewing the subject?
What are the confrontational strategies?

How Do I Determine the Intervention Goal?

The threat manager should determine the broader intervention goal for any situation, then select from a range of options for managing the Subject to achieve the goal. Obviously, defusing the risk of violence is paramount. Other goals might include solving the Subject's grievance, setting up a third party to monitor or influence the Subject, or getting the Subject mental health relief. When choosing the best management strategy, the threat manager should answer the following questions:

1 Who is the Subject and what are the circumstances prompting their behavior? The threat manager must consider who they are dealing with and the circumstances behind the Subject's inappropriate behavior.
2 Will the strategy ensure the safety of the target, other potential targets, or the public? Answering that question requires taking into account the security countermeasures available to the target. It also entails considering how the Subject might respond to the management strategy.
3 Is the strategy proportionate to the Subject's behavior? Overreacting almost certainly makes the situation worse, while underreacting may embolden the Subject. The choice of the management strategy needs to be in balance with the Subject's misbehavior. Threatening the Subject with arrest for writing an annoying letter escalates the situation, while not arresting a Subject who committed a serious crime chances making the Subject feel invincible.
4 Is the threat manager prepared to adapt or replace the management strategy in response to the Subject's reaction to it? No strategy fully

DOI: 10.4324/9781003543282-12

solves the problem, some may inadvertently worsen it. The threat manager should be prepared to alter or change strategies as the situation unfolds. Effective threat management requires flexibility.

5 Can the threat manager maintain, adapt, or replace the management strategies over the long term? Since none of the strategies promise a definite resolution, the threat manager should keep in mind the need for sustaining or replacing the selected strategy over time. The amount of effort required to keep a close monitoring on the Subject cannot be maintained over months and years, so the threat manager needs to phase in new strategies that evolve along with the situation.

Exercising a particular strategy alters the chemistry of the case. For every action or inaction by the threat manager and target, the Subject will react. That action–reaction requires reassessing the situation, the Subject, and the effectiveness of the management strategy.

What Are the Various Intervention Approaches?

Both hunters and howlers require managing. Hunters pose a threat of violence; howlers cause disruptions and may, if ignored, become hunters. Managing involves the threat manager working with subject matter experts and other involved parties to devise ways for influencing or controlling the Subject's unwanted behaviors. The range of threat management strategies available to the threat manager falls into two general categories: nonconfrontational and confrontational. Figure 10.1 illustrates the range of intervention approaches.

What Are the Nonconfrontational Strategies?

Nonconfrontational strategies either work behind the scenes without direct contact with the Subject or involve approaching the Subject calmly and solicitously to understand the Subject's concerns and, if possible, to help find a solution.

Take No Further Action at This Time

If the threat manager assesses the situation as posing no risk to the target, taking no further action means doing nothing based on that low- or no-risk assessment. This may occur either because of false or exaggerated initial reports or the Subject backs off or otherwise shows no behavior or other evidence of intending harm or further disruption. As with every management strategy, the threat manager should carefully document the reasons justifying the use of this strategy.

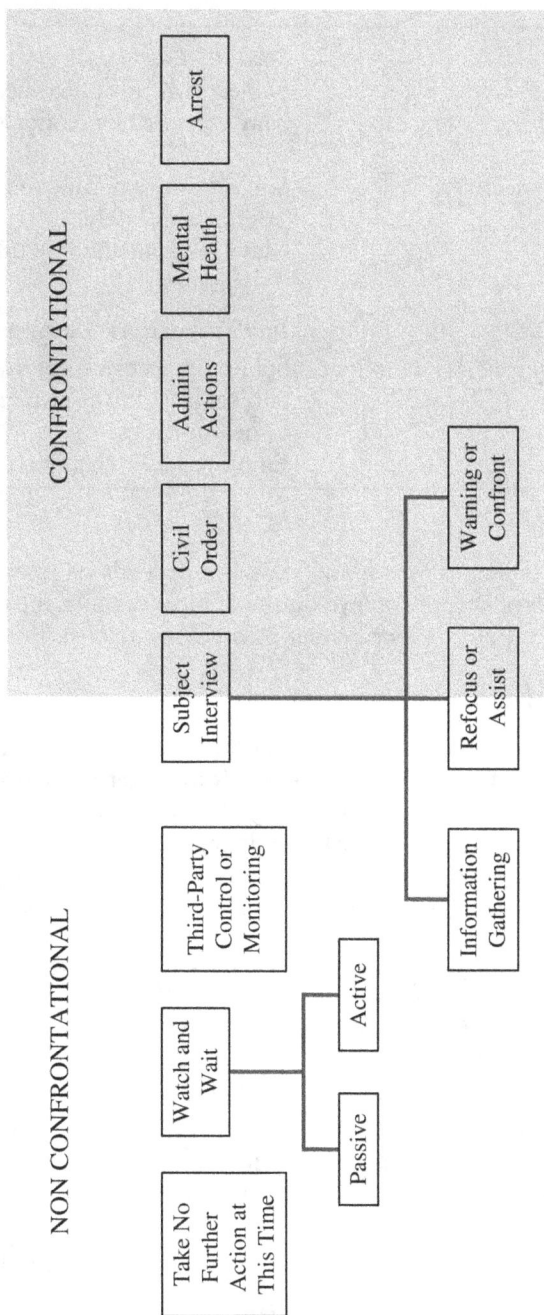

Figure 10.1 Range of Threat Management Strategies

Pros and Cons of Take No Further Action at This Time

Advantages	*Disadvantages*
Preserves time and resources	Subject controls outcome.
Avoids insulting or angering the Subject.	May escalate next contact.
Makes case inactive.	Subject may continue to act inappropriately
	May leave outstanding questions or issues.
Effective When	*Ineffective, Even Detrimental, When*
Case positively assessed no risk.	Subject expects a response.
	Subject has violent or mental health issues.
	Employed as a default strategy.

Watch and Wait

The decision to simply watch and wait also depends on a low-risk assessment. It involves keeping an eye on the Subject without their knowledge. The strategy can be employed either passively or actively.

Passive Watch and Wait

Using passive watch and wait, the threat manager keeps an eye on the Subject without them knowing that the threat manager is interested in them. This could involve simply briefing the target to ensure that any subsequent communications or contacts – whether inappropriate or not – get reported. The strategy works best in low-risk situations where further contact with the Subject may escalate the situation. For example, a Subject involved in a single incident during which they lost their temper and said or did something stupid would be a good candidate for passive watch and wait.

Pros and Cons of Passive Watch and Wait

Advantages	*Disadvantages*
Gives time for the Subject and situation to calm down.	Waiting is frustrating, especially for the target.
As a follow-up strategy, gives time to evaluate the effectiveness of other strategies.	No formula for how long to wait.
Effective When	*Ineffective, Even Detrimental, When*
Subject is a habitual howler.	Subject expects a response.
Time is an ally.	Situation is high risk.

Active Watch and Wait

Active watch and wait, as its name implies, requires the threat manager to maintain frequent contact with the target and any other involved parties in the expectation of additional contacts from the Subject. It also entails energetic information gathering about the Subject, all done without alerting the Subject to the threat manager's interest.

Advantages	Disadvantages
Avoids further provoking the Subject while continuing fact-finding and new assessments.	Target may lose patience and demand action.
	Subject may be expecting a response.
Effective When	*Ineffective, Even Detrimental, When*
Subject poses a low risk of violence.	Used in high-risk situations.
Used as a follow-up to other strategies.	Relied on as default strategy.

Third-Party Control or Monitoring

In some situations, the threat manager may identify a trusted third party with a relationship to the Subject who can monitor the Subject's activities or, in rarer cases, may exert some control over the Subject. Probation or parole officers, parents, and spouses – if they're reliable – make good candidates for third parties. Once again, the strategy works best if the Subject remains in the dark about the threat manager's relationship with the third party and the threat manager trusts that individual.

Pros and Cons of Third-Party Control or Monitoring

Advantages	Disadvantages
Uses established control systems.	Third party may mess up.
Requires confidence in third party and open communications between threat manager and third party.	Third party may become an enabler for the Subject.
	Third party may minimize or not report relevant Subject behaviors.
Effective When	*Ineffective, Even Detrimental, When*
Resources for control or monitoring are already in place.	Third party proves incapable.
	Third party believes Subject is right.
	Third party loses control, contact, or interest.

What Are the Considerations in Interviewing the Subject?

Subject interviews combine fact-finding with managing the Subject. Interviewing the Subject allows the threat manager to collect information directly from the Subject while possibly exploiting management opportunities. The interviews, then, become quite fluid and situation dependent. They allow the threat manager to gather information from the Subject, thus gaining insight into the Subject's point of view while obtaining evidence. They also offer opportunities to explore ways to stop the Subject's problematic behaviors, including finding ways to resolve the issues or, when appropriate, confronting the Subject about why their behavior is problematic.

Pros and Cons of Subject Interviews

Advantages	*Disadvantages*
Provides a direct source of information.	Risk of physical danger.
Offers an opportunity to stop problem behaviors.	May anger the Subject.
Chance to directly confront the Subject.	Potential for complaints or lawsuits.
May stop Subject's problematic behaviors, especially when they have committed no crime.	Warns Subject of threat manager's interest.
Clarifies ambiguous or confusing contact by Subject.	
Effective When	*Ineffective, Even Detrimental, When*
Subject is rational with reasonable demands.	Subject's behavior is not clearly inappropriate.
Target is cooperative.	Subject unresponsive.
	May interfere with potential prosecution.

Interviewing the Subject may branch off into three different strategies. During an interview, the threat manager may find openings to:

1 Gather information about the situation.
2 Refocus or assist in resolving the Subject's grievance.
3 Warn or confront the Subject about their concerning behaviors.

Caution

In deciding to interview the Subject, threat managers
should balance between

Watch and Wait

Or

Engage and Enrage.

Source: Gavin de Becker, *The Gift of Fear: Survival Signals That Protect Us From Violence*, (NY: Little, Brown and Company, 1997), p. 134.

Interview for Information Gathering

During an interview, the threat manager may draw out information from the Subject, thereby gaining insight into the Subject's intent, motive, and ability. The interview may also build confidence between the Subject and the threat manager, a connection the threat manager might use to influence the Subject.

Pros and Cons of Interview for Information Gathering

Advantages	Disadvantages
Gains Subject's point of view.	Potential physical risk.
Learn other information from the Subject.	May escalate the problem.
Chance to earn Subject's confidence.	Potential for complaints or lawsuits.
Effective When	*Ineffective, Even Detrimental, When*
Subject is willing to talk.	Subject irrational, irate, or uncommunicative.

Interview to Refocus or Assist

While interviewing the Subject, opportunities may arise for a positive intervention. The threat manager could refocus the Subject's attention on the threat manager and away from the target. With a bit of imagination and flexibility, the threat manager may see ways to resolve the Subject's complaint. The threat manager may also be able to develop a positive relationship with the Subject. Approaching interviews with empathy and a suspension of judgment goes a long way toward placating the Subject without harming the target or making the situation worse. Not every approach needs to be hostile.

Pros and Cons of Interview to Refocus or Assist

Advantages	*Disadvantages*
Shifts future contacts to threat manager.	Requires time, effort, innovation, and flexibility.
Assists Subject to resolve problem.	Initiates a long-term relationship.
Potential to solve the Subject's issues.	Risks raising, then frustrating, Subject's expectations.
Effective When	*Ineffective, Even Detrimental, When*
Subject's problems can be resolved.	Situation is high risk.
Threat manager is able to re-solve the issue.	Subject has unreasonable or irrational demands.
Useful when contacts are more bothersome or annoying than risky.	

More About
Ways to Help

Arrange medication, if appropriate.
Involve Subject's family members for support.
Obtain pro bono legal assistance for Subject.
Act as liaison between Subject and bureaucracy.
Encourage the use of alternative dispute resolution techniques.

Interview to Warn or Confront

Interviews also may offer opportunities to sternly warn the Subject. The threat manager may explain what might happen if the Subject continues their inappropriate conduct. Sometimes, Subjects don't understand that their actions cause fear or concern in the target while exposing the Subject to possible criminal or disciplinary penalties. When appropriate, pointing out these risks may convince the Subject to back off. However, this does not mean provoking the Subject into committing a crime such as attempted assault on the threat manager. Confronting the Subject means explaining to them the seriousness of their situation and the risks to which their behaviors are exposing them.

Pros and Cons of Interview to Warn or Confront

Advantages	Disadvantages
Might work.	Alerts Subject to threat manager's involvement.
Might prompt confession or incriminating admission.	Initiates adversarial relationship between Subject and threat manager.
Effective When	*Ineffective, Even Detrimental, When*
Subject has not committed any prosecutable offense but seems headed that way.	Situation is high risk.
Subject does not understand the seriousness of the situation.	Subject has unreasonable or irrational demands.
Sufficient evidence to prosecute and the prosecutor agrees.	

What Are the Confrontational Strategies?

Subject interviews straddle the border between nonconfrontational and confrontational strategies. Information gathering and refocusing or assisting the Subject creates a friendlier, supportive atmosphere. Warning and confronting transform the relationship into an adversarial one, with the threat manager's taking on a hostile and authoritarian stance toward the Subject's interests and goals. The other strategies on the confrontational side of the boundary increase that combative relationship.

Civil Orders

Civil orders bring in the law through court orders that address the Subject's problematic behaviors. Restraining orders, stay-away orders, trespassing violations, and similar judicial measures issued against the Subject allow contempt of court penalties for any violations. Because they do carry criminal penalties, the use of civil orders is restricted to precise and specific conditions provable in a court of law. The burden falls on the threat manager and the target to convince the judge of the necessity of the legal action. Violations, too, must be proven with sufficient evidence of the Subject's misbehavior.

Pros and Cons of Civil Orders

Advantages	Disadvantages
Relies on the power and authority of the courts.	Lengthy process requiring continuous monitoring.
	Highly provocative and therefore risky.
Effective When	*Ineffective, Even Detrimental, When*
Dealing with law-abiding individuals with significant inhibitors.	Subject's probable response is violence.
Subject nonviolent, even if violations are likely.	Court lenient to violations.
Court takes a zero-tolerance approach.	Threat manager cannot monitor the situation or respond quickly.
Immediate response ready for any violation.	Reasonable protective measures are not in place.
Reasonable protective measures are in place around the target.	Unenforced order is worse than no order at all.

Administrative Actions

Administrative actions use an organization's disciplinary process to address the Subject's actions. They include such steps as suspensions or terminations for employees and students or denial of services to clients, patients, and customers. They are organizational and bureaucratic responses involving the organization's processes and procedures.

Pros and Cons of Administrative Actions

Advantages	Disadvantages
Provides a powerful tool.	Subject to appeal and reversal.
Works through familiar control systems.	May be publicly embarrassing.
Most organizations have established processes and procedures for applying the actions.	Disrupts the Subject's inhibitors by disinhibiting them.
	Beginning of a conflict, not an end.

Effective When	Ineffective, Even Detrimental, When
Subject's behavior falls within the organization's disciplinary process.	Other elements of bureaucracy are uncooperative.
Other elements of the bureaucracy cooperate.	Treated as a solution to a problem.
Carry through can be completed.	

Mental Health Commitments

Mental health commitments depend on showing convincing evidence that the Subject is:

- A danger to self;
- A danger to others; or
- Gravely disabled.

Getting individual Subject's committed has become quite challenging due to today's competition for scarce resources. Nonetheless, for Subjects struggling with mental issues, commitments may offer the only hope for curbing the Subject's behavior.

Pros and Cons of Mental Health Commitments

Advantages	Disadvantages
Gets Subject professional help.	Initial involuntary commitment for only 48 hours.
Some jurisdictions prohibit Subjects who have been involuntarily committed from possessing a firearm.	Requires monitoring Subject's progress.
	Needs follow-up strategies.
	May require several commitments.
	Not a solution but beginning of a process.
Effective When	Ineffective, Even Detrimental, When
Subject actually living with mental health problems.	Effort to obtain commitment will not succeed.
Mental health facilities cooperate.	Used to transfer problem to another agency.

Arrest and Prosecution

When the Subject commits a crime, getting them arrested can be an effective threat management strategy, at least in the short term. In taking this very aggressive step, the threat manager must be confident that the Subject did, in fact, break the law and that the evidence supports charges against them.

Pros and Cons of Arrest and Prosecution

Advantages	Disadvantages
Subject gets incarcerated.	May fail to defuse the risk.
Law enforcement comfortable compared to other strategies.	May increase Subject's intent to harm the target.
Punishes Subjects who commit crimes.	Subject realizes law enforcement now involved.
Timing of the arrest gives tactical advantage for optimum use.	May embolden the Subject, especially if not convicted.
Effective When	**Ineffective, Even Detrimental, When**
Prosecution will result in conviction and incarceration.	Insufficient evidence.
Chance to arrange conditions on probation or suspended sentence.	Arrest will be followed by release on bail.
Subject already on parole or probation.	Subject pleads to a lesser offense.
	Nuisance-type violations resulting only in fines.

Part III

Threat Management Pitfalls

Chapter 11

Threat Management Dynamics

What are the threat management dynamics?
What are the pitfalls in threat management dynamics?
How do the knowns, unknowns, threat assessments, and protective responses interact?
What is the intervention/inhibitor quandary?
What are some of the ethical challenges involved in a threat management intervention?

What Are the Threat Management Dynamics?

Effective threat management recognizes that threat situations change dynamically. Multiple factors influence the changing dynamics, many of which lie well beyond the threat manager's control. As a result, the threat manager needs to continue to:

1 Keep gathering more information about the Subject and the situation.
2 Use the new information to reassess the degree of risk posed by the Subject.
3 Based on the reassessments, reevaluate the management strategy and the protective response.

Figure 11.1 illustrates the dynamics interacting in any threat situation.

What Are the Pitfalls in Threat Management Dynamics?

The interactions between the Subject, target, threat manager, and the intervention strategy create numerous pitfalls in managing any situation. Because of the synergy created by all these moving parts, any one of them can compound or exacerbate the Subject or the situation. The threat manager should view each situation as an unknown chemical reaction that can take off in any direction.

DOI: 10.4324/9781003543282-14

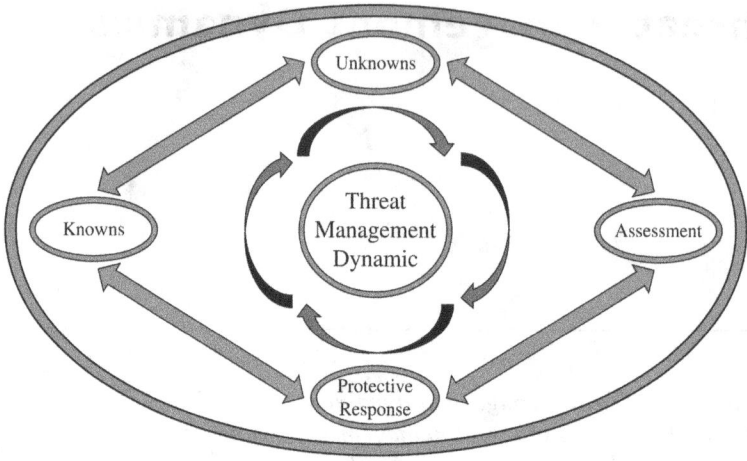

Figure 11.1 Threat Management Dynamics

How Do the Knowns, Unknowns, Threat Assessments, and Protective Responses Interact?

What the threat manager does or does not do in response to the actions of the Subject further complicates the dynamics of the situation. Taking that into account also requires reassessing the threat and reevaluating the protective response and management strategy.

Figure 11.2 illustrates the intervention synergy that results from these dynamic interactions.

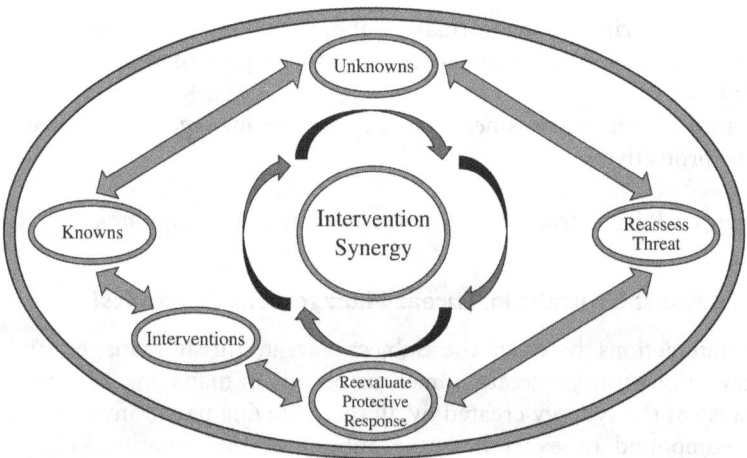

Figure 11.2 Intervention Synergy

What Is the Intervention/Inhibitor Quandary?

Balancing all these moving parts requires the threat manager, among other things, to weigh the risk of using an intervention *versus* the potential loss of one of the Subject's inhibitors. The quandary posed by that balancing act can become quite delicate. For example,

- Should an employee living with a mental illness who is potentially violent be terminated, thereby removing the inhibitors of both the job and the medical benefits that provide them counseling and medication?
- Should the school administration expel a student for making threats of violence, thus removing the inhibitor of the school structure and access to counseling while also leaving the student at home alone and unsupervised during the day?
- Should a client at a social service office be denied service due to their unruly and angry behavior, even though getting the client a job and other services could end the problematic behavior?

Each situation must be addressed individually, taking into account the specific details of the setting and its unique dynamics. Threat management offers no generic answers to these examples.

What Are Some of the Ethical Challenges Involved in a Threat Management Intervention?

Effective threat management recognizes the ethical responsibility of not redirecting the Subject to another target, except, perhaps, the threat manager themselves. It also requires not leaving or exposing others to any risk from the Subject. Nor should the threat manager use the situation to exploit some benefit for themselves, such as ingratiating themselves with upper management. The intervention should not be used to apply unsuitable or illicit pressures on the Subject, target, or situation. Finally, the threat manager should never use their position to exploit the weak in favor of their superiors.

Chapter 12

Silos

What are silos?
What is the best antidote for silos?
Why are protocols needed?

What Are Silos?

A significant challenge to effective threat management results from break-downs in communications caused by silos. Silos occur when individuals fail to share information within their organization or with other interested parties. Silos result in thwarted communications, competition between organizations, redundancy, and a higher risk of system failure. All of these are extremely harmful to any threat management program. Effective threat management relies on open and frequent communications among all interested or affected parties.

What Is the Best Antidote for Silos?

Creating and maintaining robust communication channels among all relevant parties, both within and outside the organization, offers the most effective antidote to silos. Threat managers need always to stay alert for any indication of the silo effect and the possible impact a particular ecosystem has on information flow. To offset any silos, the threat manager may have to interact with different parts of the organization or environment to make sure that they obtain all material information pertaining to the threat situation. In effect, the threat manager may have to serve as the bridge among the different silos to fit all of the pieces into the puzzle. At the same time, the threat manager needs to coordinate with outside entities that share an interest or have a stake in the situation.

DOI: 10.4324/9781003543282-15

Why Are Protocols Needed?

These communication channels should be established as a standard practice long before any threat situation actually arises. Information silos are ever present for many reasons, including legal, confidential, and logistical. That fact of life makes it crucial that the threat manager establish protocols for gathering and disseminating information as an integral part of an overall threat management program.

Chapter 13

Bunkers

What are bunkers?
What is the best antidote for bunkers?

What Are Bunkers?

The risk of developing a bunker mentality in threat assessment falls at each end of the security spectrum, from physical security at one end to threat management strategies at the other.

Physical security: Once an organization or facility puts physical security measures in place, people within the perimeter start to feel safe. As time passes, the security erodes, often by the actions of the individuals within the security perimeter. Feelings of complacency blind anyone from seeing the gaps emerging in the security measures. The bunker seems secure when, in fact, insecurities have emerged.

Threat management strategies: Intense focus on a specific target can lead to neglecting risks to neighboring targets. Protecting one's own bunker may divert the at-risk Subject toward other targets or even the community at large. By not alerting other security organizations or local law enforcement, the bunker mentality endangers other potential targets.

> **More About**
> ***False Assumptions That Bolster Bunkers***
>
> Belief that protective measures alone can fortify against all potential threats.
>   Belief that an intervention expelling a threatening Subject from an organization provides adequate security.
>   Belief that ensuring the safety of one target suffices while leaving other targets or the public at risk.

DOI: 10.4324/9781003543282-16

Many potential targets and decision-makers either deny any risk or adopt a fatalistic attitude. Deniers hold dear to the idea that since nothing has happened so far, nothing will happen in the future. The fatalists believe that if somebody really wants to do something, nothing can really stop them. Both these mindsets can be used to reject reasonable security recommendations.

What's the Best Antidote for Bunkers?

Once again, the solution, only partially effective, relies on maintaining open lines of communications and collaborating with other entities. Defusing a bunker mentality requires constant vigilance that consistently questions the effectiveness of security measures and the strategies employed for threat management.

Chapter 14

Shortsighted Intervention Strategies

What are shortsighted intervention strategies?
What is the best antidote for shortsighted intervention strategies?

What Are Shortsighted Intervention Strategies?

The concern that any action or inaction on the part of the threat manager toward the Subject will make the situation worse hangs over every threat management decision. That apprehension often paralyzes threat managers into doing nothing in the hope that the Subject never intended to act out violently in the first place. At the same time, a poorly thought out or poorly executed management strategy can, in fact, be worse than doing nothing. Demands made by the potential targets, combined with the complex nature of threat management interventions, erect significant hurdles for every threat manager. These challenges, combined with the concerns of the potential targets and the complex nature of using threat management interventions, pose significant challenges to every threat manager.

Biggest Test for Effective Threat Management

Interestingly, unclear situations pose the biggest test for effective threat management. In a small number of cases, the risk of violence clearly appears imminent and undeniable and requires an immediate emergency response. Seeing the Subject approach with a weapon in hand does not require further fact-finding or a formal, written threat assessment. Rather, that scenario requires an immediate, emergency response. In a much larger percentage of situations, the risk of any impending violent outcome appears low to nonexistent, thereby allowing the threat manager to take no further action at this time. Threat managers can readily identify each of those extremes and react appropriately.

DOI: 10.4324/9781003543282-17

Greatest Challenge for Threat Management

The situations falling in between those extremes pose the hardest challenge for effective assessment and management. The facts may be murky or insufficient to support either a high- or a low-risk assessment. The threat manager's working environment adds further complications by imposing certain rules that control or influence the threat manager's responses. Corporate bureaucracies often have little or no patience in dealing with problem employees, especially when the easiest course is to follow the corporate disciplinary process. Yet, doing so risks making a bad situation far worse. Law enforcement often measures its success rate by the number of arrests and not by how often they defused any risks, even though arresting the Subject may escalate their determination to react violently. Schools opt to suspend or expel unruly students. In doing so, they then lose all influence and oversight over the Subject.

Pressured Into Shortsighted Decisions

These pressures often compel threat managers to make shortsighted threat management decisions. The demands of supervisors or upper-level managers, lack of resources, impatience, and easy access to familiar bureaucratic ways all conspire against making the best threat management decisions.

What Is the Best Antidote for Shortsighted Intervention Strategies?

The only antidote to shortsighted intervention strategies draws on the threat manager's skill, experience, and flexibility in making assessments and deciding on the best management strategy. By maintaining strong lines of communication within the threat manager's organization, the threat manager can bridge bureaucratic divisions and foster a cooperative environment. The best counter to avoiding myopic intervention decisions is to anticipate future actions and reactions, rather than focusing solely on the here and now and what is immediately to the front. Carefully considering all the potential disruptions and counter-reactions – in effect, consciously accounting for all the things that can go right or wrong – helps prepare the threat manager for any contingency. This differs from playing the "What If?" Game because it is rooted in reality and based on what is actually happening. Realistically and factually anticipating the Subject's possible reactions to a threat management strategy differs entirely from imagining all the things the Subject might be capable of doing. Doing so also provides the threat manager with persuasive arguments defending the threat manager's recommended intervention strategy. Avoiding shortsighted intervention strategies requires deliberately and thoughtfully taking in the big picture and then explaining why the recommended strategy fits best within that picture.

Chapter 15

The Golden Rules of Threat Management

I. Keep in mind the circumstances and context in which the Subject acts when assessing and managing the Subject.
II. Measure the impact of the *Intimacy Effect* on the Subject.
III. Reassess whenever a threat management strategy is applied, new information emerges, or the Subject changes their behavior.
IV. Take no action or inaction likely to prompt the Subject to act violently.
V. Be flexible and innovative in managing the Subject.
VI. Always be mindful that hunters hunt and howlers howl.
VII. Never mislead the Subject or promise them more than you can deliver.
VIII. Be respectful toward the Subject by upholding their dignity.
IX. Avoid the "What If?" Game by keeping to the facts.
X. Continue managing the case for as long as the Subject poses a risk of violence or disruption.

DOI: 10.4324/9781003543282-18

Index

Note: Page numbers in *italics* and **bold** refer to figures and tables, respectively; and those followed by "n" refer to notes.

For Product Safety Concerns and Information please contact our EU
representative GPSR@taylorandfrancis.com
Taylor & Francis Verlag GmbH, Kaufingerstraße 24, 80331 München, Germany

9 781032 895260